Discovering YOU

Discovering YOU

✢ ✢ ✢

An Eloheim and The Council Book

Channeled by
Veronica Torres

First edition June 2012
ISBN: 978-1-936969-30-2

Copyright 2012 Veronica Torres
Eloheim.com

Published by Rontor Presents

Cover Art by Holly's Creative Design
Hollyscreative.com

Interior Design by Mary T. George
Epubpub.com

Contents

Introduction

Out of the hundreds of private sessions I have done, this is the first session I have offered as a book. Kay's concerns and challenges are so universal. There are so many people who are "drained from doing too much" and can't find the answer to the question, "What am I here to do?" I knew before the session was even finished that I was going to offer this material in book form.

The insights and tools Eloheim offered Kay are such a wonderful road map to transformation. I am thrilled to present it to you.

I want to thank my team, Mary George, Sue Trainor, Dea Nicholls, and Holly Eve Adams for their contributions: formatting, transcribing, editing, and creating the artwork for this book.

I especially want to thank Kay. Her openness and willingness to look her challenges right in the eye was incredible to witness.

Step by step, transformation and healing are ours!

Blessings,
Veronica

June, 2012

From Kay

Eloheim is a straight-talking, humorous resource for my soul and for any and all who feel lost within themselves. I was questioning within my being who I am as an essence, and my place in this world; this session helped guide me to the important spark of light and influence that I emanate…! (As opposed to the sometimes random feeling of being just another cog in the wheels of life.)

Eloheim as channeled through Veronica helped point my feet in the right direction.

This information, while simple in its wisdom, had a profound effect on me claiming my birthright as a divine co-creator of my wildest dreams!!

Thank you Eloheim,
Kay

Session Transcript

Eloheim: Hello! Where do you wish to begin?

Kay: I wrote a couple of things down.

Eloheim: We're going to interrupt you because we're looking at your energy. Your energy field is at 10% of optimal. You're run down. You're really run down and you're contributing to being run down by—how to best say this?—let us just get the right feel into it. When you start to get run down you do not set boundaries soon enough. We suggest people set boundaries early and often and you are not setting boundaries anywhere soon enough to keep your energy level high. This is why you're tired. This is why you've had weight gain. This is why you feel this midlife crisis kind of energy. You've let yourself run down so far that you're on fumes and then, when you're on fumes, because you're trying to fix it, you fix it by trying to do the things that ran you down in the first place only more, better, faster. This idea of, "I'll just do three plays instead of one and that'll make me feel better because I'll be doing stuff." Right?

Kay: Right.

Eloheim: We're looking at your energy field right now and instead of your aura being four feet outside your skin, it's inside your body. Your truth, your radiance, your emanation, the part of you that everybody who knows you thinks is so delightful, that big smile and that beautiful energy you have to offer is inside you. It's not even coming out right now. It's not getting past your skin. When we see that and see you in this condition it's a 9-1-1. It's a stop the presses. This has to be corrected before anything else is addressed. There's a question we're going to ask you: Why are you afraid to emanate your truth to this world? Where does the survival instinct have its claws in you? Where does fear have its claws in you? What is the big, bad, boogie man that's telling you to stay small?

Kay: I don't know.

Eloheim: You don't know. We know you don't know. That's why this has happened to you, because you don't know. What we see happening is that over time you've given with your performances, you've given with your abilities, you've given with your massage work, you've given with your vibrant personality, that sense of giving, giving, giving, giving as a way to feel connected to the world. So when you give, give, give to be connected to the world, you give away your wax, you give away your essence. The option that we suggest for you and for everybody else is to emanate.

There's a huge difference between giving and emanating. Emanating is knowing what your truth is and letting that shine out of you. Giving is trying to figure out what other people want and trying to figure out a way to offer it to them. All you're required to offer to the world is your truth experienced. Not looking around in other people's energy to see what it is they want and then trying to give it to them. Here's an example from your acting career: You don't poll the audience to hear what play they want to see. "Who wants Hamlet, who wants this one, who wants that one? Okay, everybody, it seems like we're going to have to do a mishmash because no one can agree." You don't do that. You say, "This is the play. Come and see it if you want to." You want to connect to the audience and you want to give them a powerful experience, but the truth of the matter is you're having your truth being presented. "Take it or leave it, like it or don't. I don't give a shit because I know I'm coming from the authentic version of me."

Instead of emanating your truth, what you're doing in your life is asking everybody what play they want to see. If you don't know the lines to the play they request, you say, "I don't know the lines to that play, oh well, I'll just try anyway." Then, you don't feel success, you don't feel confident, you're always what we call on your toes instead of your heels. When you're on your toes you're leaning forward into other people's energy fields, snooping around. When you focus on feeling your heels underneath you, it lets you feel the truth of you *for you* and it shoots out into the world with an extraordinary powerful effect that's none of your frickin' business. None of your business at all. What your business is is committing and recommitting to knowing what your truth is in any moment. "I'm tired. I feel taller today. I feel fatter today. I feel skinnier today. I feel like my husband is a kook today. I feel like the dog is happy today. I feel. I feel. I feel." If you can't figure out what your truth is, ask yourself, "What is my left ear doing? What's my right toe doing?" Which brings your self back to the body, back to the moment, back to your awareness. And then what happens is you get connected to your intuition, your soul, your guides, so that you can start having new thoughts instead of using the hamster-wheel mind to think all the old thoughts over and over again, which is what you've been doing. And you don't just hamster wheel thoughts; you also hamster wheel the behavior of giving instead of emanating.

You're always looking for ways to give to others, but you're not giving from your abundance. You're giving from your reservoir. And it's run way down. You've got to stop that because it is not healthy for you. When you're in the world and someone says something to you, you need to say: "What is my truth in this moment?" And when you express your truth, don't apologize for it being your truth. State your truth. Shut your mouth. We call it short, factual statements. State your truth. Shut your mouth. If you feel triggered like: "Oh, what are they thinking? Am I letting them down? Blah, blah, blah." Say instead, "I don't give a shit. Because right now my number one focus has to be rejuvenating my reservoir, by emanating my truth and not giving away myself."

You deserve this. If you don't do it for yourself, no one is going to do it for you. We know that you wish to have a positive impact in the world; however, you won't be available to have any impact on anyone because you won't be healthy enough. You just can't fuck around with this. Your energy is so low. Normally people we see like this, we think something is wrong with their thyroid. We don't think something is wrong with your thyroid right now. We think you're just at 10%. You know like when you drive your car and that light comes on because you know you need gas and you keep driving and you're wondering, "Will I make it?"—you're in that place. Right?

Kay: Yup.

Eloheim: You know this is the truth. So what are you going to do about it? How are you going to change it? You are going to walk on your heels. Literally. Pay close attention to your heels. When you know where your heels are you know where your tailbone is. When you know where your tailbone is you know where your shoulders are. When you know where your shoulders are you know where your head is. When you know where your head is, it's with the rest of you and not in other people's business. Because that's the real temptation even of light workers—especially light workers actually, because light workers want other people to do well, be happy, blah, blah, blah. This is really come to a crux point for you.

Kay: Yeah, oh yeah.

Eloheim: This is part of that whole thing you were talking about regarding a midlife crisis. "I have been giving, giving, giving, for forty-seven years." And part of what happens is you're so busy giving that your emanation doesn't get to have its day in the sun; and your emanation is actually the powerful force that you came here to share, but it's corrupted by the idea that you have to give and that other people are more important than you. You see this with your husband—the two of you are excellent mirrors on this subject. You see him give too much and know it's not a good idea. Every time you see him do it, we want you to recognize, "My internal world creates my external reality and my husband wouldn't be behaving this way if it wasn't also true in me." By changing it in you, you energetically allow him to change as well—if he chooses to—because he doesn't need to continue to model that behavior for you. He may continue to experience it for himself, but you'll have a completely different reaction to his experience of it. By emanating an option you show him how you can actually share the beautiful people that you are without running yourselves into the ground.

You do this by catching yourself over giving and saying, "I give to myself only. And then I emanate as my gift. I give to myself only and then I emanate as my gift." Then people are blessed by your presence, which is what you've always wanted, and you're fueled because you continue to give fuel to yourself. Without this you will not be healthy—and we don't mean to scare but we're trying to scare you a little. We don't want to freak you out but you can feel it in your body. You feel uncomfortable with your size. You feel uncomfortable with your energy level. You feel uncomfortable with your ability to get up and go.

Kay: Totally.

Eloheim: It's because of this situation where you're giving instead of emanating. Giving results in such a small amount of energy being shared with the world. Emanating offers a supernova of energy to the world. But you have to let go of the belief that the only way to have an impact on the world is to make sure the people you encounter are happy with you.

Kay: Oh my God, totally.

Eloheim: Right?

Kay: Yeah. I don't even realize I do that. It's subconscious at this point.

Eloheim: One of the things we've been teaching in our weekly sessions is to discover the places you're unconscious you're unconscious. Part of the reason to attend the weekly sessions is you get to spend an hour and a half every week focused on discovering these aspects of yourself so that you don't make the kind of choices that lead you down this path of feeling so drained. It helps you stay on top of it more. And then, of course, at the meetings we're there and if we look at you and say Kay, you're doing better or Kay, we see you doing more giving than you did last week, it helps you to not give yourself away.

Kay: It's been an ongoing issue. Do you see some certain intuitive abilities that I could tap into that could be developed?

Eloheim: Sure. If you would do this emanating thing instead of this giving thing, it's going to leave this big space in your life and that big space in your life can be reconnecting—because this isn't something that's lost—it's just reconnecting to the intuitive abilities that you've always had and you've always known you had. So this is how the pattern goes: Kay gets an insight from her soul. Kay looks around into the world to see who she can give it away to. Then Kay feels drained.

This means that insight from your soul is connected to feeling drained instead of insight from your soul being connected to feeling good. You get an insight, you feel, "Oh, yes, I feel like I have some energy in my body." And you don't necessarily give the specific insight away, but you give away the reservoir that you've built by connecting with your soul's insight. You get an aha and that fuels you and you immediately give that fuel away to someone by wanting them to feel good.

You know what? People will feel good when they see you feeling good. Right? You watch Veronica walk around in the world and you can see she's doing well, you feel good because she's doing well, even if she hasn't talked to you in a month. That's emanation. That's the difference. Can you feel that difference? This is a good model for you. Emanate your truth. Receive insight. Yes, absolutely. Intuition? Absolutely. You have all of that. And you can play with it when you're not filling your life with giving, you can play with it more and ask yourself questions and say, "Hey, that's an idea!" You have that power in you and you need to make room for it by giving up the other pattern that does not work. You've already done that for forty-plus years. You've learned enough about that. You're an expert at how to do things that way. Let's gain expertise in something else.

Kay: That's where I'm at too. Ready to learn new things.

Eloheim: Emanation.

Kay: So if I start emanating more, is it possible if I continue to do massage work that there's a way that I can take it up a notch, and do some tarot card readings or something? I need to step into my power and emanation, but …

Eloheim: Exactly. Start with that. Start with when you go in to do massage. Instead of feeling like you have to make a certain experience for the client, instead say, "The vessel of massage is going to be the way I emanate my truth."

Kay: So the technique itself...

Eloheim: This is a really triggering place for you to make this change, because massage is all about making the client have a good experience; but the truth of the matter is a client can get a massage from anybody, but when they get a massage from you they're getting an opportunity to be in your emanation. If you're able to get on your heels—which doesn't mean you don't give a great massage—it means you're on your heels when you're giving the massage and you're being in your truth rather than being in, "I wonder what they're thinking, I wonder how this is coming across, do they like it, what else can I give them?" They end up being bathed in your emanation and when your emanation is conscious, high-vibrational, angelic, it's a healthy feeling, it's a confidence, it's that quiet centered place that almost nobody knows how to access in this world.

When someone comes into your massage room and you can greet them in a very centered way, you're already offering them healing. If you can stay in a very centered place the entire time you're offering the treatment, you end up giving them an emanation to match, rather than a little bit of a positive experience for an hour and then they go off to their busy life. When a high-vibrational, powerful, light worker generates an emanation into the world, it says to everyone they encounter, "There's another way to live." It's not: "Read this book, go to this meeting, do this thing." It's: "As I walk through the world I'm showing you there's another way to live that's not the way that the world says to live." It's magnetic and very attractive and you can offer that in your sessions as a starting point of broadening what's going on. And people will come just for that, and they even would come to lie on your table without receiving a physical massage.

Kay: Yeah. Yeah, yeah.

Eloheim: Not because you're doing something to them or giving to them. It's because they're basically basking in your emanation. It's a lot like when you encounter someone who's a saint. The saints that you grew up with in the church—you know that if all you did was sit in their presence you'd be changed. That's emanation. They don't have to do a thing. You just sit there and you feel changed. That's the difference. Now we feel you feel it. That got there.

Kay: Well, that answers a lot.

Eloheim: It's good to have specific questions because then we can talk about how to apply it. So don't hesitate to claim this time as your own and ask what's important to you.

Kay: Okay, good. The emanation, that actually really does solve so much of this. I'm kind of blown away. So I was offered this directing opportunity to direct another children's play. It could be something different. Is it worth my time and energy? I get paid very little, but obviously if it is a chance for me to be in my emanation—I'm looking for ways to transcend this old me and get to that emanation very quickly. A quantum leap.

Eloheim: Well, you have to keep in mind that emanation is happening right now. So it's not something you have to get to. You just have to remind yourself to focus on it. It's like the train is going down the tracks and they've thrown the switch and you can go this way or that way. It's a fundamental change that doesn't require a quantum leap. It's a fundamental change that results in a changed destination. So if you do the play, the question is why are you doing it?

Kay: Yeah.

Eloheim: Because obviously the money is a token amount, so it's not to give you affluence or comfort in the money situation.

Kay: The one thing I thought of was the girl I'd be working with—we've worked really well together, and if there's a future for me in children's theater, she's just a great person to work with so it could be aligning with my future to work on it.

Eloheim: Oh dear. So the reason you're doing it is another person. You see how you do this? We asked you why you're going to do it and you're talking about this great other person. You see how you do that "we" thing? You've got to really watch that. It's forty-seven years of training so it's not like we're criticizing you. We're just saying for forty-seven years, the garbage can has been on the right side of your desk and you're moving it to the left, so it takes a little bit of time to get used to. But you have to be so disciplined with yourself. So back to the question, why would you do this? Answer with an "I" statement. I feel (blank) when I'm the director.

Kay: I just can't believe it. I feel like I've got to do a song and dance. [She is covering her mouth with her hand as she speaks.]

Eloheim: Don't cover your face. Don't cover your mouth. When you do, you are saying, "I can't tell my truth. I have to cover my mouth when I speak."

Kay: I feel scared being a director by myself.

Eloheim: Okay, now we're there. I feel scared being the director.

Kay: It's not something that comes right to me. Because my whole life I've done exactly that. It started with my sister who was a very demanding personality, and I gave away my power then and I'm just seeing the whole thread here. It's unraveling everything.

Eloheim: So I feel afraid or scared when I'm the director…

Kay: But it should be an empowering experience.

Eloheim: No, no. One of our least favorite words is the word "but." You know what happens with the word "but"? You tell your truth and you put a "but" in it to modify it for the audience. "I feel afraid when I'm directing, but I shouldn't. I like red pants, but I only bought blue ones."

Kay: I do a lot of that.

Eloheim: The truth is before the "but," and the stuff after the "but" is very fascinating because that's the "make it socially acceptable" side of the statement. When you find yourself using the word "but" be really careful because you're modifying your truth.

Kay: Honestly though, I feel that way about a lot of stuff right now. There's the idea of going back to college and is that the right choice?

Eloheim: So let's ask. I feel (blank) when I think about going back to college.

Kay: I feel intimidated when I think about going back to college.

Eloheim: I want to go back to college to get (blank).

Kay: To get confidence and competence so that I can actually prove to the… Ah, see, there I go again.

Eloheim: Very good! You caught yourself this time. And you didn't cover your mouth as you said it! See how the questions you're asking are based on other people…

Kay: Oh my God.

Eloheim: It's the royal "we." It's the big "they." It's not "I." It's not Kay. It's not what Kay's truths are.

Kay: I have to find my niche. I'm going crazy. I have to find my niche in this world.

Eloheim: Your niche in this world is you and your truth emanated.

That's what it is. A lot of light workers come on to the planet and think, "What am I here to do?" We say over and over again—and we really do say this to everybody, not just you—you come here to emanate your truth. You come here to connect with your soul's perspective so you can emanate even more of the grander truth of you than the human body has been able to emanate up to this point. "I come here to grow, to emanate my truth and I'm an actress and I'm a day care worker and I'm a nanny and I'm a chef and I'm a wife and I'm an auntie." And the common thread—your niche—through the whole thing is: I emanate my truth no matter where I go or what I'm doing.

Kay: That is huge. Thank you.

Eloheim: That is your big thing.

Kay: I found my niche!!!!

Eloheim: That's why you're here on the planet. Although you have the ability to be so shiny, yet you are not shining right now because you've been so focused on giving instead of being a gift to yourself. It's not judgment, it's not criticism, it's just opened eyes, more awareness, need to make a change, how ridiculous does it have to get before I make the change? Not any more ridiculous than this. You at 10% energy is as ridiculous as we want this to get. We don't need you flat in the bed.

Kay: That's what I've been doing—seriously—I've been watching *Little House on the Prairie* episodes and taking naps. I don't even know what I've been doing. I've just been absolutely drained and feeling just really lost. Like I don't even know where to go from here. I don't even know who I am any more.

Eloheim: That feeling right there encapsulates what we've been explaining. You don't know who you are because you've given away your reserves, so really you're kind of empty. The beauty is that now that you're aware of it, you can recharge and you'll not give away again. It's going to be a temptation when you're with your family and all those kids and your husband and your clients to go back into the old pattern. But the truth of the matter is, you see and know that that is not right for you.

The alternative here is to allow yourself the ability to be the mother that you always wished you had, be the mother that you thought you might want to be in this lifetime, to yourself. You are your own child. Loving yourself as much as you wished you had been loved, as much as you love your nieces and nephews, and as much as you would have loved being a mom yourself, that amount of love that you have to give to another you need to give to yourself. And the way you do that, we just want to remind you, the way you do that is to check in and ask, "What is my truth, what is my truth?" And if you can't figure out what that is, ask, "What is my big toe doing? What is true now about my left index finger?" Literally ask that. "What is true about my left index finger?" It might sound silly, but it brings you into the moment and it tells you what's going on in your body. When you get in touch with your left finger, you may realize: "Oh man, I feel sad. Or you know what? I don't feel as sad as I have." So what is your truth right now?

Kay: My truth is trying to figure out how to stop that pattern. I know it goes back to emanation, so I'll keep that as my mantra for a while until I start feeling it on every level. But I'm so concerned, how do you stop being concerned about letting people down? My boss was amazing—I worry about my boss sometimes because we have such a connection and then I'm worried about cords and making cords with her.

Eloheim: You are doing the same thing as when we asked you about being a director and you told us about the girl you worked with; your truth is about other people. They're more important than you. Basically that's your thing. Everyone is more important to you than you.

Kay: So how do you get there?

Eloheim: You just have to keep reminding yourself: "Oh, there I am." We love this tool we have called I'm tempted to. "Wow, I'm tempted to think about my boss's feelings more than my own.

I'm tempted to think about nurturing another person more than deciding if the play is right for me to do." And when you put the words "I'm tempted to" in the thought, it makes you, literally, use a different part of your brain. So you're not using the part of your brain that's very habitualized to that idea. It lets you use a completely different part of your brain, which is exactly what you need. So, "Wow, I'm tempted to think about my boss right now." And then you know it's a choice because you're a creator. "Is my choice to think about her and if so why? What is my thinking about her going to change in me?" We even just said to you, "What is your truth?" Now the answer to your truth could be: "I feel sad right now, I feel uncomfortable right now, I have to pee right now"; but it was this flowy dramatic kind of truth. So we're going to ask you again: "What is true now for you, Kay?"

Kay: Well, actually…

Eloheim: I…

Kay: I feel like I need to cut everything out right now, to be honest with you. Because I just feel like if I go into my husband's world, I'm going to be doing open mics and art projects and that's a scattered thing; and he's asking, "Why aren't you singing with me?" And if I go into my boss's world she's like, "Why aren't you looking at your phone every five minutes and see if you have a massage?" So, just to be honest, I just want to be free from all of it for right now and get back to that emanation. I don't even know where to start but I think that what would help is to just mentally…

Eloheim: Energetically, not mentally.

Kay: And even tomorrow I was supposed to go in on Easter morning for a meet-and-greet read-through of this play I've already done, and I'm even wondering if I should do that.

Eloheim: So the way you do all these things—two things we want to say. The first is we have a tool and it's the "Say no first" tool. If anyone asks you for anything or to do anything, you say "no" first. You just say, "No." If someone says, "Do you want to do this?"

"No." "Can you go here?" "No." "Are you available?" "No." You just keep saying "no." Once you've said "no," there's breathing room for you to actually check in with yourself to discover how you really feel. It makes room for you to take the time to authentically determine your truth about the question. Once you've checked in with yourself, you can always change your mind. We've actually never seen anybody use this tool and then change their mind and not have it received well.

Kay: That's it. It's wonderful.

Eloheim: So you just say "no," and the funny thing is how fast you get to say "no" can be really entertaining. Like the person hasn't even finished asking and you're saying, "No." So you can have fun with it. You were wondering about making decisions—this is going to help, the "Say no first" tool.

Kay: That's going to really help because I am horrible sometimes with decision making.

Eloheim: Yeah, and you've got a husband who's even worse than you. The "Say no first" tool is a really good one for both of you. And the thing here, Kay, for you, is when you want to make decisions you've got to learn to carve out the space where you are checking in with yourself first. The "Say no first" tool really resonates with you, right? So tomorrow's Easter morning, and they want you to go do a play rehearsal on Easter morning? What is your truth about that?

Kay: No.

Eloheim: See how that works? "I don't want to."

Kay: I already told her I had plans, but I was going to try to make it.

Eloheim: See how you hedge your bets? So here is how you're going to do it. "No," and then you go: "Wow, I'm really tempted to feel guilty, confused, uncertain, I suck, I'm letting her down."

Kay: Totally.

Eloheim: But you know what happens? We're going to tell you a little secret here. When you set clear boundaries early and often, you give permission for others to do the same.

Kay: It is so wonderful. I love it when people say no. I love it.

Eloheim: So you say no first and have fun with it. When you have triggers because you've said no, you use the "I'm tempted to" tool to interrupt the trigger pattern. Then you're using a different part of your brain. The other tool that's going to help you is the Short factual statement tool, because you tend to be very thespian about your thoughts. If it can't be done in three paragraphs, it shouldn't even be started. I need pages to work out this feeling. You have to watch that. It's good for the stage, but sometimes sucky in life.

What we want you to do is use the Short factual statement tool, which means that you speak about things with a short factual statement ended with a period—and you say the word period because that makes you use a different part of your brain. Imagine you're hamster-wheel thinking about: "Should I go to play practice tomorrow." Then guilt: "I suck, I let her down, blah, blah, blah" happens.

The "I'm tempted to" tool and Short factual statements go really well together because you can say, "I'm tempted to go there but instead my short factual statement is, I don't want to go, period." Because if you just say, "I don't want to go," you're just using the same part of your brain over and over again. If you say, "I don't want to go, period"—and this is the most important part of this tool—"I don't want to go, period"—then you sit in that opening you have created and you see what new information comes in.

You don't just put period in between each sentence to hamster-wheel think. It's not: "Oh God, if I don't go she's going to blah, blah, blah." It's: "I don't want to go, period." And then you sit in the period and say, "I'm tempted to feel guilty about that, period." Where do you go next? "Wow, if I don't go I'll feel guilty," or maybe: "Wow, I feel really relaxed that I don't have to go out tomorrow."

We have seen this tool cut hamster-wheel thinking that has lingered for three years down to two or three rounds of the period thing. You have to be super careful that at the period you don't just keep thinking the same old thoughts. That you stop and say—especially for you—stop sign. I'm at the stop sign. When you come to the stop sign in your car what do you do? You evaluate the intersection. You don't just stop and then go right away without looking, because you might be crashed into. You stop and evaluate the intersection to see what the next step is. When you use the Short factual statement tool, imagine you're at a four-way stop when you say that period; and you stop and you look around before taking the next step or thinking the next thought. Take what you have observed and make another short factual statement based on the new place you are in.

Kay: Yeah, I love that. I am so mental and I'm just constantly—a hand analyst took a look at my palm one day and she said, "All you do is think. You never get anything done because you're always thinking everything through." So this will really help that. The hamster-wheel mind totally makes sense because it is those patterns and that continuous thing.

Eloheim: Work with the "I'm tempted" tool and the Short factual statement tool together to create an empty space so you can rediscover yourself. We really want you to become friends with the current version of you because we don't think you know who she is. She's this amazing woman who's grown and learned and been married and had businesses and had friends and done plays and all these adventures; but you haven't actually gotten to make good friends with her yet because she's never present long enough, as she's always giving away to somebody else. Another thing for you to keep in mind is: "Who is the current version of me?" And not: "What am I going to do with her? Where are we going to go? What thing is next? Should I do that play or not?" It's: "Who is she?"

We have another tool for you. This is the Step-by-step tool. Step by step. You take a step and it's like that stop sign thing we were just talking about. You re-evaluate. You make another step, you re-evaluate. You go step by step. The key here is, with the step-by-step tool, if you feel confused about your future, you're making too big of a step. When you make too big of a step, the survival instinct jumps in and grabs a hold of you and says, "Be afraid, be afraid, be small, be small" and you don't get anything done.

Kay: Ahhhh, that's what's screwing me up. Oh, I love that! I love the step-by-step method. Because that's what I've been feeling like. I'll make this step and something will stop and I get really confused by it because I keep projecting way out into the future.

Eloheim: This is what we call the Moment, or the mountain tool. One time, a client was telling this big long story. She's going on and we imagined her walking and the next thing we knew she was clear over there on that mountain. Energetically, she was that far from the moment. We told her, "You're over there on the mountain. We're over here in the moment."

Kay: Wow!

Eloheim: This big long story you've told us has taken you away to the mountain way over there. We're over here trying to help you, but you're not even close to us. What we've found is that story-telling creates more surface area for the survival instinct to grab a hold of you. When the survival instinct grabs a hold of you it will say, "Stay small because if you change it might kill you. What you've done so far hasn't killed you yet, so don't change because you might get dead."

The survival instinct very adamantly doesn't like you to grow spiritually because it requires too much change. When you're on the way to the mountain, you're wearing a meat suit for the saber-toothed tiger of the survival instinct to come and find you. Come back here, come back here to the moment, to the current version of you, to short factual statements and I'm tempted, to saying no, to doing step by step and taking even smaller steps and what is true now? What is true now? Tell us, what is true right now for you?

Kay: Right now this moment I'm starting to feel some clarity, which is great. As a matter of fact I thought to myself just now whether I should go to college, I should just drive to the JC. Just take that first step and see. Because I do have that guidance and I will be guided and I'll get those instincts and aha's. So that really helped.

Eloheim: Bring it back. And then just bring it back. That's far enough into the future. And a good answer to what is true now is, "I like the taste of my gum."

Kay: I see. Even that present.

Eloheim: That's fun. Because that's a smaller step. If you imagine, you were going to take a stride, what nerves, what muscles have to twitch and tingle before the foot can actually lift. That's what we mean by small step by small step is to recognize that even to lift the leg and move it forward six inches— so many things happen before the foot even leaves the earth. So you can back into yourself—get back on your heels—back into yourself enough to where you can have that kind of awareness. Back into yourself so you can have that kind of awareness.

Kay: I'm just thinking again that a lot of my questions have been answered, especially if I just stay in this step-by-step way of approaching life, but...

Eloheim: There's a but, so be careful. That's another important concept, we call it "but and because." Whatever you were going to say after the "but," have great suspicion about, because it's not necessarily going to be your truth. What were you going to say?

Kay: I was going to say but...[she catches herself and laughs]

Eloheim: Veronica can barely type it in an e-mail anymore so you're in good company.

Kay: Going with the energy of kind of who I am, can you see a certain route for me to follow?

Eloheim: With what desired outcome? Knowing that outcome is one of our least favorite words. Be really careful here! You used "but" and "outcome" in the same sentence, watch out! [laughter]

Kay: I did get to a truth the other day. Believe me now with the step-by-step method I really can see how it's going to work itself out but—not but.

Eloheim: "And" and "however" seem to be good words to try in place of "but."

Kay: The flow is much better. And I was thinking the essence of what I really want is that feeling of stardom and with that word "emanate" I got it. My boss was helping me with some class ideas with the kids. My hesitation is around the parents, but again that's fear stuff. However, if I really do follow these steps a lot of that will be taken out because I'll be speaking my truth and emanating my truth.

Eloheim: And people will feel more confident around you because you'll be showing your confidence.

Kay: That's really the essence of what I've been going through with this midlife crisis thing. There was a part of me that was like, "Oh, yes, I know exactly which role to play. Okay, are there injuries or ailments? I'm there for you." And pouring out—the Aquarius with the pouring water. And then I'd feel like Dr. Jekyll and Mr. Hyde. I want my own business. I don't want to work for anybody anymore. And I've been saying that. I want to be specialized, and then on the other hand I've been, well, it's so safe. This idea of emanating is really helping me with everything. There were two other questions. I think once I start emanating again, I think it'll help me drop my weight. A lot of my friends are doing weight-loss programs and counting points, which drives me nuts. I've also read about not dieting and getting rid of emotional eating, which I tend to do. So I've been teetering back and forth. Do you see one that would flow better for me?

Eloheim: What we see you doing is that you are trying to preserve yourself by adding weight—because imagine the water pouring, giving, giving, giving, at some point your body says we have to hold on to anything we have just to stay alive. Survival instinct. That's reptilian brain shit there. When the body gets this drained like you've been, the body says, "Nine-one-one. Every calorie we have to hang on to. We can't expend it. We have to hang on to it. We can't burn it." So that's why you get depressed and don't want to move around—because the body is saying, "Don't exercise, for God's sake! We don't have any to spare. You want to be skinnier? We're trying to stay alive here." So yeah, you don't have to do a weight loss program. Just watch your emanation. You don't have to count any points. You just have to use the tools, I'm tempted to, short factual statements, don't say but, say no's, and do step by step. That's what you need.

Kay: I started picking up that learning how to channel book. I'm wondering if I have the capacity to do that.

Eloheim: At some point you may be ready to have a conversation of that nature, but right now it's way premature because you have to get your energy back up before you can give to anybody in any capacity. You do have an interesting connection to non-physical energy and we will address that with you at a later time when you come to us and you're at least 90%. We won't talk to you about it until you're 90%. So that's something to keep in the mind that there's…

Kay: I have a goal now.

Eloheim: There's more to be talked about when we get the human thing working a little more correctly.

Kay: I really, really appreciate that.

Eloheim: Because you really do. We're not trying to hold out on you. If we give you any more information about this you're going to think about that instead of thinking about what you need to think about. It would be like, "But if I could just …" That's another word we don't like, "just." "If I could just"—"but," "just" and "outcome"—we get annoyed with the word "because," too; however, "but," "just" and "outcome," you have to be really careful about those.

Kay: The other question is what is a good way to clear up karma, especially if there's somebody that you felt a connection with and they just keep popping into your brain and you want to push them aside and they just pop in again?

Eloheim: A really important thing to do is to say, "What is my truth about this thing popping into my brain? Am I using it to distract me from this moment because this moment is uncomfortable? Am I using it to remind me of a different time in my life that maybe I feel some kind of connection to?" We feel like for you it's mostly a way to get out of the moment.

Kay: Yeah.

Eloheim: It's a romanticized thing about getting out of the moment. And romanticized things can sometimes be romantic and can sometimes just be drama—like the princess trapped in the tower kind of romance. So in essence you're kind of the princess trapped in the tower.

Kay: Yeah, that's it. You just hit the nail right on the head.

Eloheim: We're sort of good at that.

Kay: The other kind of karma is where you left somebody in the dust. Is there a way to clear that up?

Eloheim: We call that relanguaging. So you say, "Okay, the woman I am today wouldn't have ever done that. The woman I was then was doing the best she could in the circumstances and I won't repeat that pattern."

Kay: It doesn't mean I have to come back in another life? If I come back again, I want to be walking on water or something.

Eloheim: Well, we shoot for walking on water in this lifetime.

Kay: Me too! That's one of the reasons I'm here.

Eloheim: Once we get you tuned up a little bit, you'll have a better shot at it. We don't suggest you try now.

Eloheim: So is there something else you want to throw in before we wrap up?

Kay: The last one is theater and spirituality and how that's an ongoing—I'm always pivoting back and forth.

Eloheim: It's because of the emanation thing. You feel like: "I'm in my truth when I'm feeling spiritual and when I'm in the theater, I'm giving, giving, giving and not being in my truth." You don't get to feel like you're in your truth in all moments because you have been kind of wearing a costume. So as you get this emanation thing figured out you won't feel like you have to make choices between. Can you feel that?

Kay: Yes, I can and thank you.

Eloheim: Practice, practice, practice makes perfect on this. Remember, it's forty-seven years of habit you're trying to change.

Kay: Thank you. I love it! I've got homework! Thank you.

Eloheim: It was fun working with you.

Tools

Big toe, left elbow

This is a great tool for bringing you into the moment. When you find yourself pulled into the past or the future, ask yourself, "What is my left knee doing? What is my big toe doing? How does my tongue feel? If I touch my teeth what does that feel like?" Asking what your body is feeling short-circuits the temptation into thinking about the past and future. The key is once you've thought about your elbow and short-circuited the temptation into the past or future, to then let go of thinking about the elbow and allow yourself to stay in the moment. Then, open to insight from your soul by saying, "What's really going on here?" If you find yourself getting tempted away from the moment, repeat the tool, "What's my left elbow doing? What's my big toe doing?"

When you use this tool, be sure to use a body part that you don't normally think about. This will make it even easier to avoid habitual thoughts.

◆◆◆

Veronica writes:
I love the tools that make me smile when I use them. The inquiries, "How does the back of my knee feel?" or "What is my right eyebrow doing?" make me feel light and joyful, which I'm sure helps me sink

even more deeply into the moment. This fun tool is easy to remember and quick to apply.

◆◆◆

Focusing on my big toe reminds me that I can point my feet in any direction I choose.

—Denise

Candle wax (Nobody gets your wax)

This tool is based in an analogy: You are a candle. You can share your flame—your emanation—but you cannot give away your wax. Never, never, never, never. If you give away your wax, you give away yourself, and who you are is diminished.

If you're a candle, you can light numerous other candles with your flame, but nobody gets your wax. On some level, we see you energetically very drained because your wax has not been precious to you. That core amount of attention, of rest, of nourishment, of peace, of quiet, of meditation, of walking, dancing, whatever it is that you know feeds you as a person and keeps you whole. You've been letting pieces of those things go to other people because you thought, "Well, if they're happy, I'll be happy." Or, "If they're happy, at least I won't be so distracted by their needs." When the truth is, you've gotten yourself drained and you'll get further drained. So, step back and set boundaries. Boundaries don't mean: "I don't love you anymore." Boundaries mean: "I have to love myself first, so I have extra love to give. I can't give from this place. I have to give from a whole place." If you keep giving from weakness, eventually you have nothing left, but if you set boundaries, you rejuvenate yourself.

The first step is to set boundaries so that the people you're giving your wax to don't get any more. And they usually throw fits, so you have to deal with that. They'll call you selfish, typically. Or they'll call you a bitch.

When you drop service mentality and take care of yourself first, you're able to offer something extraordinary. It's the candle. The candle is lit and the flame is giving off light. It gives off light whether you hide it in a closet or you set it on your windowsill. And when you love yourself well, it's like putting the candle on the windowsill so the people who are driving by see the light as well.

You can give your flame to anyone because it still burns even when you share it with others, but when you start giving your wax away it's all over.

◆◆◆

Veronica writes:
This was one of the early tools and it is still very much in use. It is so very easy to get pulled into "service" and siphon off your wax. I know what that feels like and I am not going back there! It is such a joy to focus on emanating my truth and knowing that that is all the "service" I need to do.

◆◆◆

Habitual response of codependency felt seamless until I heard this tool. My sense of global responsibility burdened me in a way I thought was my identity as a "responsible person." I felt guilty about not being able to help all women feel safe, for instance. Imagining myself as a being who has limited physical shape (the candle as my body) with unlimited consciousness and intention (the flame), I saw imme-diately that the love and attention I choose to offer a situation flows from a source that is constantly renewable. When I have used as much of my physical energy to support my intentions as I have available, I must rest without shame. Actually, to rest with relish, enjoying the dreams that replenish insights and creativity.

—Margy

◆◆◆

The candle wax tool is very good for me as I have a tendency to go out of my way to help others, sometimes to great lengths. So, the idea of sharing my flame and not my wax made very good sense to me. It's helping me to be crystal clear on when I may be stepping over the line and when I need to reel it back in.

—Joseph

How ridiculous does it have it get?

How ridiculous does it have to get before you are willing to change a habit? How much suffering must you experience? How many times do you have to experience the same patterns?

How ridiculous does it have to get? The answer? Usually, pretty damned ridiculous.

You're constantly putting up barrier after barrier after barrier to taking responsibility for your creation because the habit of victimhood is so strong in you. Sure, the choice for consciousness is challenging, but suffering is painful and repetitive. Owning "I did this" might be hard, but what is the alternative?

Don't require it to become ridiculous before you are willing to transform it. If it has become ridiculous, then transform it immediately!

◆◆◆

Veronica writes:
When it gets ridiculous, I KNOW whatever it is must move to the top of my to-do list. I must stop and become as conscious as possible about what is going on and what I am experiencing. When it is ridiculous, I bust out all the tools until it isn't ridiculous anymore!

◆◆◆

I remember this tool when I notice things building to a frenzy and

chaos begins to reign. It reminds me to get conscious quick—and often leads to a bout of laughter!
—Randy Sue

◆◆◆

How ridiculous does it have to get? This tool is actually somewhat soothing for me. Living in a foreign country with a busy schedule and acclimating to new standards and rules, many interesting and exasperating scenarios pop up daily. At one point, I was writing them all down because I didn't know what to do with them and all the emotional responses that were getting triggered. With this tool, I can be amused. I can laugh more. And it helps me focus on what I get to look at—on why this is happening FOR me, or what is the VELCRO here, who is answering the door, why this is in my lap—it is a personal inner adventure more than an external chronicle of events.
—Anna R., Mexico

I'm tempted to...

"Tempted" is one of our favorite new words, as in "I'm tempted to go into fear. I'm tempted to be angry. I'm tempted to stay small here. I'm tempted to be uncomfortable." Before acting or reacting, insert "I'm tempted to" into your thoughts. This will break the habit of immediate responses and, instead, allow you to recognize that you have a choice of reactions.

This creates profound transformation. Why? Because it gives you the opportunity to leave the fear-based operating system. Instead of reacting with the first emotion that pops up, you can use the consciousness-based operating system and realize, "I'm actually comprehending this moment rather than habitually experiencing this moment."

As an example, when you choose to say "I'm tempted to be afraid" rather than just reacting in a fearful manner, two main things happen. One, you actually use a different part of your brain. You can imagine your brain saying "Oh wait, we're not going to just think the same thought today?" The second thing that happens is your thoughts pause, giving you a moment to realize the truth that you create your reality; it jolts you into a position of, "Oh wait, this is a choice."

Inserting "I'm tempted to," will bring you much more deeply into the moment and take you out of hamster-wheel mind obsessive thinking. The thing we like most is how it stops your thinking and centers you.

You can really stretch this tool. Try it out: "I'm tempted to brush my teeth right now." "I'm tempted to make the bed right now." "I'm tempted to put on my shoes right now." Using the tool this way will help you see how much of your moment-to-moment behavior is running on autopilot and how much of it is chosen consciously.

We love this tool; it does so many things all at once.

♦♦♦

Veronica writes:
This is a powerhouse tool. It really, really works. I remember when Eloheim first introduced it. I found myself saying, "I'm tempted to" all the time! I began stretching out the words when I said them, "I'mmmmmm teeeeeeempteeeeeeeeeeed toooooooo" to really bring the point home. This tool will rock your world.

♦♦♦

This is a great tool. I'm chuckling now even as I write this. The joke is you are just tricking yourself and it works. For example, you get cut off in your car by someone and you say, "I'm tempted to be really ticked off at this jerk." You are ticked off, but just by saying, "I'm tempted to" makes it surreal and funny which disperses the energy on it. This really works!

—John M., Sonoma, CA

♦♦♦

I'm tempted to is a great tool! I find it especially helpful when dealing with two of my major triggers – anger and money. I work with as a wine consultant and have many conversations with the public. I am frequently (though much less frequently than I was previously) tempted to become angry or short with my customers as our consultations wear on and their insecurity about wine causes them to become defensive, haughty, and rude with me. I simply take a deep breath and say to myself "I'm tempted to retaliate for your rude behavior –but I will not. I will recognize your insecurities and fears around wine even if you won't and I will not use anger or similar aggressive behavior to exploit the situation."

I use the I'm tempted tool on myself when I see that, once again, I am scraping the bottom of my checking account. I'm tempted to get angry with myself. I'm tempted to tell me that I suck, that I have no self-control, that I will never have any money, on and on and on. But, I acknowledge the tendency and replace those thoughts with what is true now, which is, I have enough money in my pocket for this moment and money comes to me in infinite ways.

The choice, the responsibility, and the possibilities rest with me and become my creation. It's incredibly helpful to present myself with choices in the moment!

—Rene

♦♦♦

I love the I'm tempted to tool. It allows me to voice the pattern I'd like to avoid falling into, and it gives me the room to then choose something more evolved, more in line with my growth. That acknowledgement of where I feel habitually drawn to go but decide not to is a very sweet and generous and loving gift to myself always and to the person I'm talking to, if I'm using the tool in a conversation with another. Thank you Eloheim!

—Anna

Moment or the mountain

When something occurs in your life, you may be very tempted to "tell a story" about it.

This is especially common when you can't interact with or get clarity from the other people involved in the situation. How many times have you wondered, "Why did she say that?" or: "What is he doing?" When you ask yourself questions about the behavior of others, you typically create a "story" to answer those questions.

The "story"—rather than the truth—is then used to interact with the experience; the story is typically is based in fear and built using assumptions and habits.

When you use storytelling to explain your world, you're energetically walking away from the present moment into the mountains in the distance. Storytelling does not explain your world. It just occupies your mind. If you allow yourself to stay in the moment, abide in any discomfort that you may find, and explore what is true now, you have the opportunity to experience the moment, the place where change can actually happen.

An important reminder: The further out of the moment, the more of the survival instinct you must contend with. The survival instinct says, "Keep doing what you have always done as that hasn't killed you, change is dangerous!" When you think, "I want to start a business," and you jump to: "Oh but wait, I need a five-year plan, I don't know what it'll look like, or how will I find clients?" the triggered survival instinct will be very loud. Quiet this aspect of the survival instinct by staying in the moment.

♦♦♦

Veronica writes:
This tool was created during a private session. Eloheim was gazing out a window as a client was "telling a story" about something going on in her life. Eloheim told me, "She is really far away, it's like she is way over there in those mountains in the distance." This is what allowed Eloheim to see that, when we tell stories, we leave the moment; thus the moment or mountain tool was born. I love when tools are this visceral; it makes them very easy for me to remember and use.

♦♦♦

This was my session and it was impactful in many ways. What I was moving away from in the moment was suffering. Suffering as explained by Eloheim was my attachment to wanting a different outcome to a situation, a relationship. Over on the mountain were all sorts of distracting explanations from the truth that was so painful to hear. Yet the encouragement to stay in the moment helped me not to be so unkind to myself, not to judge myself in lack or judge the other person. Eloheim added a comment that the suffering felt very "achy" to him. This recognition and acknowledgment helped me move back to the moment where I could finally separate a natural grieving of loss from the messy and useless emotions of "what if" and "why."

—Mary Y.

♦♦♦

When Eloheim introduced this tool, I recognized the habit immediately. "Storytelling" was a habitual technique I used to "process" an uncomfortable event. I would run a whole conversation through my mind in great detail about what I could have, or wished, I had said. The imaginary conversation only fueled my emotion and I never actually said the things I would say in my imagination. I recognized this as hamster-wheel thinking. This tool helps me reveal the reason I'm telling stories about the past or future so I can experience the discomfort and discover the truth.

—Mary T.

"No" is a complete sentence / Say "no" first

This tool allows you to set a boundary or state a preference without feeling the need to justify or make excuses for your position. You are not responsible for others' reactions to your choices. Stating a preference is an act of free will.

A fascinating way to learn about boundaries, preferences, and "What is true now?" is to say "no" first. Just give it a try! Someone calls you up and asks you to go out. Say "no" first.

If you are habitually saying "yes" to keep other people happy, try saying "no" and see how it makes you feel. The result we have seen is that being able to just say no is incredibly liberating. Importantly, it gives you the time to actually find out how you feel. When you say no first, you can then consider your feelings on the matter without the pressure of having the question hanging over your head.

If you decide that you actually do want to participate—because YOU want to, not just to make another happy—you can always call back and say you changed your mind.

And "No, period" is a complete sentence. You don't have to explain. There is no need for a lie, an excuse, or even other plans. If you are asked, "Why?" you can just say, "It's just not right for me."

If they don't respect that, well, that is something very good to know about them, isn't it?

◆◆◆

Veronica writes:
Oh yeah, NO… who knew? When I started saying NO first and then giving myself time to check in about how I felt, my life changed. What else is there to add?

Relanguaging

When you talk to yourself or others, make sure that you're not speaking from a place of low vibration or sharing your thoughts in a habitual way. Instead, allow yourself to relanguage what you're saying from a high-vibrational, conscious perspective.

Observe yourself when you are speaking and watch your energy. Do you feel depleted? Do you feel bored? Do you feel anxious? Do you feel repetitive and dull? Oftentimes you are like this because you're telling a story or describing something habitually. You are not actually infusing the conversation with the present moment.

Example: Don't forget your keys! relanguages to: Remember your keys.

This relanguaging focuses on what you *do* want rather than focusing on what you *don't* want. This is a powerful change of energetic.

Example: Why did I say that stupid thing? relanguages to: Next time I'm in a similar situation, I will say this _____.

This relanguaging puts the focus on the experience you desire rather than reminding yourself of what you don't want to experience.

When you're ready to express something, check in with yourself and make sure your words are reflective of your current truth, the current moment you're in. When you use high-vibrational, conscious, present words to talk about something that's real in you, it will profoundly change your experience.

This tool works with memories too. If something is plaguing you, you can re-language the way you speak to yourself about it. At a minimum, you can relanguage "Why did I do that?" to: "I did the best I could as the person I was then and I know that as I grow I will be able to handle similar situations in a more high-vibrational way."

◆ ◆ ◆

Veronica writes:
This tool is great for shifting the way you speak to yourself. If you find yourself in an obsessive thought pattern, relanguage it and watch things change. It's quite amazing.

◆ ◆ ◆

I have gotten very clear about the power of words and the affect they have on people and probably the world too. I recognize that I need to use the relanguaging tool to raise the vibration of my emanation by carefully choosing high-vibrational words when I communicate.

—Mary T.

Short, factual statements

Your brain is accustomed to thinking a certain way and it tends to continue to think the same way unless you intervene. Spiritual growth and other types of transformation require that you think in new ways. We often refer to this as rewriting the neural pathways. One of the ways we've found to help you rewrite your neural pathways is to use the tool we call "short, factual statements."

Here is how it works: identify something that you wish to change in your life and make a short, factual statement about it that ends with a period. Don't follow your statement with a "but" or a "because," and remember, we aren't doing short, factual paragraphs!

Make sure that the short, factual statement is grounded in the moment. Your statement should be about how you're feeling and what you're experiencing now.

Always end the short, factual statement with the word PERIOD. Adding the word "period" at the end let's your brain know that you aren't just thinking the same thoughts you have always thought, but that you are doing something new.

Immediately after making your short, factual statement (followed by the word "period"), observe what you are tempted to think about next. Our experience is that you will start thinking about the past or the future, or both.

It is extremely important that you catch yourself here and observe the temptation to leave the moment rather than just start to re-think your habitual thought patterns. Make a short, factual statement about the thought you are tempted to have. Now observe where your thought patterns want to take you. Continue making short, factual statements in this manner.

You are not making a short, factual statement to get an answer to a problem; you are making a short, factual statement in order reveal habitual thought patterns. You are using short, factual statements to identify the static that is clogging up the moment. Once the static is cleared, you will be able to access the moment and your soul's insight about the situation.

AN EXAMPLE:

Eloheim: What is something going on that you would like to change?

Response: My back hurts.

Eloheim: Your habitual thinking pattern would be something like this: "Oh, my back hurts, oh God, it's going to be so hard to go to work tomorrow. Oh, I don't think I'm going to sleep well, oh, I wonder if it's because the bed is no good. Oh, I wonder if it's be-cause I'm stressed out. Oh, my back has hurt for so many years, oh, it's probably going to hurt for so many more."

A short, factual statement is: "My back hurts." Short, factual state-ments are stated in the present tense. This is an incredibly impor-tant part of this tool. You have to say it in the present tense. It's not: "God, I've really been bummed out in the past because my back hurt." That's not what we're shooting for. You want to ground the <u>tool</u> in the moment. "My back hurts."—first step. Then, im-portant, but funny, step. We always try to throw in a little humor wherever it fits. "My back hurts. Period." And say the period out loud. The reason you say the period out loud is because that is actually what makes your brain get on notice something new is happening. If you just say, "My back hurts,"—you've said that a million times. "My back hurts, period," gives your brain an excla-mation point. It says to your brain, "Something new is going on here. Something is happening. My back hurts, period." And if you can do this out loud, or at least under your breath, that helps, too, because then it's not just more mind chatter. It's literally being put into your reality. So, "My back hurts, period."

What happens within you after you make that short, factual statement?

Response: Just memories of weeks on end of pain and not being able to do what I wanted to, and having money issues because I couldn't go to work.

Eloheim: Perfect. This is what we were trying to get at. So, all those fears and memories and "Oh, my Gods" come up and you are tempted to obsessively think about them again. Once you have spent some time in the past, you will typically start thinking about the future. Your habitual thinking patterns don't give you access to the moment and the moment is the only place anything actually transforms. Using short, factual statements will help you stay in the moment and actually change your experience.

Going back to our example: "My back hurts, period." Say your short, factual statement and then just wait and see where you go. Continuing with your example, you went into, "Oh my God, I might not make enough money because I can't work."

The key here is to hold yourself in the moment by making short, factual statements about what's true right now. So, you say, "My back hurts, period." And then you watch. "Wow, I'm tempted to go into the past, period." And then you watch, "Wow, there I go off into the future, period." Then, eventually, what happens is that the past and the future cannot hold you because you've made short, factual statements about them rather reuse the old neural pathways and habitually think about the past and the future.

That's the magic in this, when you acknowledge the temptations that seek to pull you out of the moment, the temptations lose their power. So, it's not: "Oh, God, I'm such an idiot, I thought about the past and the future again." We don't play that game, ever. It's short, factual statement about what's currently going on, and then short, factual statements about what comes up when you acknowledge that. Remember to keep your short, factual statements focused on what is actually occurring now. What ends up happening is you experience the moment in a new way and you can attend to what's happening from the current-moment version of you.

KEEP IN MIND:

When you realize you have something you want to change and you make a short, factual statement about it, be really, really careful that you don't expect the short, factual statement to give you the answer to the "problem." That is not the role of the short, factual statement. The role of the short, factual statement is to reveal the habitual thinking that is blocking insight coming to you about the "problem."

The temptation is to say, "My back hurts," and expect the short, factual statement to make your back stop hurting. The role of the short, factual statement in this example is to illuminate what you are actually thinking about when you experience back pain. When you become clear about that, you will be able to actually address the back pain without the baggage of the habitual thoughts getting in your way.

ANOTHER EXAMPLE:

Question: My weakness in computer repair is working on Windows 2000 servers. I don't get a lot of practice. So, I got a lucrative contract with an attorney. I did all the easy things first and then today, I had to deal with the server. So, I'm trying to research and I can't find a solution, so I start to panic. I get that feeling like, "I'm no good; I'm an inadequate technician."

Eloheim: So, a short, factual statement would be: "I can't find this answer, period."

On some level what you've been telling yourself is you have to have the answer or you suck. And by using a short, factual statement of what is really true—"I don't know the answer, period,"—what it does is takes away all of that sort of sticky, oohy-gooey stuff that's saying: "If you don't know this answer something's wrong with you." It just brings you to the truth of the matter. "I don't know this answer, period."

So, when we say that to you, what happens inside you?

Response: I'm not exactly sure what happens. What happens is that I...

Eloheim: Wait, don't think about this. If you say, "I don't know the answer, period," what happens inside you?

Response: Well, when I looked at the question I wanted to go backwards into, "You don't know and you're going to look like an idiot, and when they find out that you don't know they're going to lose respect for you." Totally into the past!

Eloheim: This is what we were saying. Typically, you go to the past first. Maybe not every time, but this is what we're seeing. You immediately thought 3, 4, 5 things. See how fast there are so many things there? The key here is not to run with any of those but instead to say, "Wow, I'm tempted to feel very insecure right now, period." And if you say that, what happens next?

Response: Um.

Eloheim: Are you thinking about it, by chance?

Response: I'm trying to feel what's going on in my body!

Eloheim: Let's not think quite that hard. What comes immediately to mind when you say, "Wow, I'm tempted to go into the past," or "I'm tempted to be insecure?"

Response: Just feeling the feeling in the gut.

Eloheim: We're picking up that it's something like, "Well, yeah, I'm tempted to be insecure because I should be." It's like, "Well, of course I feel insecure, I should feel insecure." And that's the point we're trying to make. The "Yeah, I should feel insecure," how helpful is that? Not very helpful. That's not going to get you to the answer. Abiding in insecurity is not going to get you to the answer. But abiding in "I don't know," abiding in the question of the situation, opens you to insight. Abiding in insecurity—all it does is get you more insecurity and then spirals you down. And that's why with the short, factual statement tool you're constantly saying, "Wow, I'm still tempted to be insecure, I'm still tempted to be insecure," until at some point the charge of that temptation to be insecure, it kind of gets boring, so you stop going there. Chances are, you'll eventually go to, "God, these people are going to really think I suck." You're going to go into the future. And it's like, "Wow, I still don't know the answer and they're going to have a judgment about me." Which doesn't bring you any sort of solution, either. See, that is what we're trying to alert you guys to. None of that is solution material. All of that is distraction material. All of that is taking you out of the place where you can connect with insight. Because it's lowering your vibration, it's putting you in the past or the future, where nothing happens.

A thing to also say would be: "I am ready to receive insight, period." Short, factual statement, and see what comes. We suspect you might go to, "There's no insight, there's no way, I'm not going to get it." Just rephrase that to, "Wow, I'm tempted to think there's no such thing as insight, period." You just keep bringing it back to acknowledging the truth of what you're doing. Acknowledging the truth of what you're experiencing. Short, factual statements based in the now followed by the word period. Remember, it's not about: "Oh, God, I've yet to figure out the solution." It's: "I'm training myself to live in the moment and open to insight and not be distracted by the past and the future, not be distracted by insecurities and low vibration, not be distracted by fears and lack and judgment, but to stay in the moment and to train myself and to train my brain that this is the place where answers come from."

Response: Yes, I agree.

Eloheim: We're so glad you agree.

Response: I can't hear the answers until I get to that space where I'm not afraid. It wasn't until I just lightened up on myself about it and thought about two things: So what if they do think I'm incompetent? And maybe it wouldn't be so bad if I just told them I don't have a lot of experience with Windows server but I think I can do it.

Eloheim: Or, "Maybe I need help. Maybe for this one little part of this job I could ask for help." Maybe it's OK that you don't know everything. Because at some point when you say, "I don't know anything," it means "I don't know everything." And "I don't know anything and I don't know everything means I can let myself off the hook." And it also means that it's OK to open to insight because if you think you know anything and everything then at some point you're like, "I know everything, I know enough, I'm smart, I've got it, I've got this handled, I don't need any help," that whole thing. Now, you're going, "Wow, it would be interesting to know more when I need more." And that's really what we're also looking at in this.

And it's not short, factual solutions. Don't get all heady about this. Something like, "I am in a state of insecurity but I will be moving out of it immediately," or some woo-woo talk like that. No. Tell the truth about your body. Tell the truth about what you're doing. Tell the truth about the experience you're having. And this is where the shadow thing really comes into play, too, because sometimes, what you're going to make a short, factual statement about is something that you never would've admitted to yourself six months ago.

You were pretty honest about how you felt really insecure, but another thing that you could've said is: "and I feel like I'm cheating the guy," or "I feel like I'm a liar because I said I could do the job and I can't." You could go into more shadow and that's OK, too, because what you're doing is you're making short, factual statements about it, not living it. You're taking the high-vibrational aspects of the temptations to the past and the future to illuminate what you're really doing now. What you're really doing now is acknowledging that you don't have to know everything and feeling OK doing the part that you know how to do, asking for help—whether it's from your soul or from some other technical person or Google—to do the parts that you have left and seeing if you deserve a lucrative contract when you don't actually know every single thing.

◆◆◆

Veronica writes:
I can't begin to count the number of times I have used this tool. This one is like an icebreaker ship! It breaks through to the heart of the matter. When Eloheim first explained it, they said it was the most powerful tool they had given us to date. They turn to it time and time again during our meetings. I turn to it time and time again as well. This is one powerful tool, PERIOD!

◆◆◆

Every time I use this tool it grounds me in the moment with the truth of what is going on with me at that time. It's a great tool for getting to the meat of the current issue and it quickly brings consciousness into play. It also stops the hamster-wheel mind from taking off and going down a path that's not helpful or healthy.

—Randy Sue

◆◆◆

When I am really in any kind of jam or fighting with a friend, Short, factual statements gets me straight out of the messy drama. It breaks down the issue into manageable little pieces. Working with this tool for only a few minutes, or a half an hour, I come to the "truth" of me through insight. Minimal effort with maximum results.

—Denise

◆◆◆

Short, factual statements help me most when I feel fear from an unknown location. A simple example would be going outside at night across my property, which is a few hundred feet. I have occasionally felt uncomfortable like someone or something was watching to do me harm—too much television when young. Having the Short, factual statement tool really helps neutralize that, as I say, "I feel a little afraid of something, period." Then, "Is there a saber-toothed tiger within pouncing range, period?" I answer, "No, I don't believe so, and I don't have much to fear, period." That usually works just fine. I don't really feel very vulnerable these days, but if I happen to, I say, "What the heck am I worried about? I create my own reality and I create a safe place to reside, period."

—Rosie

◆◆◆

This allows me to cut through the crap of habit; habitual response. It allows me to act in the present instead of the past or future.

—Mike

◆◆◆

I find that when I am faced with situations and people that trigger me, Short, factual statements becomes my best friend. If I am angry, instead of flying off the handle, losing my temper and allowing myself to indulge in potentially hurtful behavior, I will use a short, factual statement like: "I am really angry about _____." Then I don't say anything else—I let the other person respond. In many instances, the other person is spoiling for a fight and is relying on me to lose my temper so that we can really have at it. Well, the 2011 version of me doesn't do that, she responds with short, factual statements. I let the other person rant until they demand an answer or interaction from me and then I respond with another short, factual statement. This can go on for a while but not as long as an actual fight, and certainly with much less wear and tear on me!

The first time I tried it, I was totally afraid of what the outcome might be. I was not sure that I could hold to short, factual statements alone without indulging in argument and screaming. I had never not re-sponded in kind during one of these engagements. I was petrified that I would be beaten down with words, which had always been my secret weapon, but never yielded a satisfactory result. I knew I had to try using this great tool. I was actually shaking inside. But it didn't turn out that way—the other party exhausted their verbal anger rather quickly (to my surprise). I couldn't believe it!

The entire time I had to notice my habitual responses to the other person's anger and baiting words. I was shocked at how often I had to reframe my responses and quiet my mind to a non-reactive state. I had to be one hundred percent present in her anger and my own. I had to take complete responsibility for my creation in the moment. I was completely amazed as I realized that a recurring pattern that had been in place for almost 40 years had been broken simply by using short, factual statements. This has been a super-powerful friend and ally ever since.

—*Rene*

◆◆◆

I'm not very good at remembering this tool, which is a shame because Eloheim said it would "change your lives." When I have remembered to make short, factual statements about what I am experiencing, it immediately brings me out of the habit of thinking about the past or future and into what is happening right now. I can handle the present; I can't do anything about the past or future. It's a big relief!

—*Mary T.*

◆◆◆

This tool is phenomenal, especially for an obsessive like me! When I say that "period" at the end, I stop. There is no thought for a moment. It's like my brain doesn't know what to do with this. The thoughts that come next are usually just, "Wow, this is really interesting. I can feel it all over my body." It does interrupt the obsession with the past or the future, at least for several moments, and I can feel my brain jump to a new pathway with a more conscious thought that I choose.

—*Joy*

◆◆◆

Having been on the spiritual path for the last 25 years or so, I was guided to contact Veronica and Eloheim through a radio interview I heard. I wanted to know why, with all my hard work, etc., nothing was really changing in my life. I was focusing on nothing; the fact that nothing was changing and expecting the change to come from outside not from within. Now one could say, "No wonder you're in status quo."

During my session with Veronica and Eloheim in November of 2010, Eloheim advised me to watch all of my thoughts and when I found myself habitually thinking make a statement regarding those thought patterns and end the statement with a period. Watching every thought for three days, I started to feel my entire consciousness shift. My entire being opened up to more experience and being more in the moment. The part that is so amazing and so unbelievable is that it is very hard to describe, for that past part of me seems so distant and so far away.

I cannot imagine myself habitually thinking or feeling my life is so limited. My life is more and more in the moment and more and more opening up to all that is there for me.

—Anthony

Stand on your heels

The act of standing on your heels is really powerful. We probably never would have come up with this tool if Veronica hadn't started wearing high heels. When she did, it changed the way she walked in the world as she realized, "I always have to be aware of where my heels are — literally where my heels are in my shoes — or I will fall down." When you have to be so aware of where your feet are or you might fall down, that will bring you into the moment! It's great.

This tool isn't just for women! It would be great for everyone to at least try on a pair of high-heeled shoes to get a physical sense of what we are talking about.

When you're aware of where your heels are it aligns your body — physically and energetically. Then it allows you to experience your current, in-the-moment self. This also keeps you from leaning forward into other people's business, leaning forward into the future, or leaning forward into outcome.

Stand on your heels and you will find yourself more deeply in the moment.

◆◆◆

Veronica writes:
When I first started wearing high-heeled shoes, I didn't have a clue what I was doing! I always felt like I was on the verge of falling on my

face. I finally realized that I was putting my weight and my attention on the balls of my feet which left me feeling off balance. When I shifted my attention to my heels, a whole new world opened up. It's a powerful way to walk in the world. I like it so much I don't want to wear flat shoes anymore! It's so much more fun to walk on my heels in my heels!

♦♦♦

When we do standing poses in yoga, our teacher reminds us to ground through the heels into the pose. That is where the power and strength of the pose originates. It makes total sense to me that Eloheim would tell us to stand on our heels. The strength and power of a grounded stance is useful not only in yoga but in every facet of being. It has been my experience that when I am not walking and interacting in this way, I am likely to be off balance, not in the present moment and even out of the body. So yes, stand on your heels is great for any occasion whether you're wearing high heels or no shoes at all!

—Rene

♦♦♦

A simple and powerful tool. When I walk around slumped a bit and looking downward, my thoughts go to the past or the future. I find when I lean back and put more pressure on my heels I feel as though I am emanating my truth. It opens my chest, straightens my back, lifts my head and I'm ready to experience the moment. My thoughts are quieter as I simply experience the truth and the sweetness of now.

—Mary T.

Step by step

You are changing so rapidly and you're dropping habits so frequently that if you're not reanalyzing how you feel about the path you're on each time you make a step, you could be missing out on a change of direction that would facilitate your having even more of what you want in your life.

Each time you take a step, allow yourself to check in and say, "I know I'm a different being now that I've made this one step. Let me reevaluate if continuing in this direction is still valid or if perhaps, now that I'm different, it's time to change direction."

Remember to take very small steps. If the survival instinct flares up, if fears flare up, if uncertainty gets ahold of you, if you're very confused, you're taking too big a step. You're "biting off more than you can chew." Take a smaller step. Steps can be very, very, very small.

An example of a small step is to check in with your body. Ask, "Am I hungry? Am I thirsty? Have I had enough rest? Have I had some fresh air today?" Sometimes you get so projected into the future that you lose sight of what the body needs in this moment.

We have a visual that can help you remember this tool. Imagine that you previously saw your life path as a line of stepping stones heading away from you. Now imagine that this picture includes stepping stones in radiating circles all around you.

As you take a step onto a new stone, stop and acknowledge, "I know my compulsion is to go straight ahead, but what does this stepping stone – meaning this moment – inform me about where I wish my journey to go?" Don't assume that you need to continue to step in the direction you were previously headed. With each new step, you are a new person. As that new person, reevaluate the direction you, as the new person, wants to go.

Don't rush. Move piece by piece, step by step. Piece by piece, step by step. You don't need to speed ahead. You don't need to jump. You're not racing toward conclusion. It's moment, moment, piece, piece, step, step, moment, moment. Each little step is a place of aliveness and fascination. It's: "I'm here in this moment and then I'm integrating what this moment gives me. And then I'm here in this moment and I'm integrating what this moment gives me."

In the past, the habit has been to run from step to step, just gleaning what little you could to fuel your step onto the next stepping stone. Now it's step, integrate, evaluate, move. Step, integrate, evaluate, move. Step, integrate, evaluate, move.

❖❖❖

Veronica writes:
This tool is a sanity saver! I realized that I was taking WAY too big a step and I was very off balance so I wrote this little poem to help me remember this tool.

> *Take a big step*
> *Be upset*
> *Step small*
> *You won't fall*

It sure helps me!

❖❖❖

The visual of radiating circles as opposed to a straight path ahead helps a great deal. The goal of linear processing via the straight-ahead path seems to be attached to Expected Specific Outcome, like a college degree or a particular dress size. And we all know what happens when we seek a specific outcome. Step by step can seem slow to overachieving light workers, but it's actually taking off limitations if viewed as the circles of potential.

—Mary Y.

◆◆◆

To help me remember to take even smaller steps, I changed my password to stepbystep2. This is not easy to type quickly! But it was a really good reminder to take it easy and go one step at a time – before dashing off (mentally, physically, or emotionally) into the world. I've changed it to something else now, but I may change it back again as needed.

—Rene

◆◆◆

For me, this tool is a reminder that change sometimes happens slowly in small steps and that that is okay. There is plenty of time and no need to be mean to myself because I haven't mastered a new skill as yet. Even small steps reveal new layers of the onion of my consciousness.

—Mary T.

◆◆◆

For so many reasons including to feel safe, I used to try to plan things at least five years in advance. I was in overwhelm mode all the time, stressed and unhappy. The step-by-step tool reminds me to pull back, evaluate where I actually am, not where I THINK I want to be and take my projects and my life one moment at a time. When I take things step by step, I relax more and actually stop and smell the roses along my way.

—Randy Sue

What is true now?

Asking yourself "What is true now?" is a way of staying connected to the moment and your soul's insight about the moment.

It's fairly easy to remember to say "What is true now," but it's also very easy to be habitual about the answer you allow yourself to experience. What is true now is not answered by the mind. What is true now is answered by an "aha" from the soul, so by asking yourself what is true now constantly, you're creating a very strong connection between you and your soul, which is a fine thing to do if you're interested in transforming your life. The truth of you must be experienced consciously.

If what is true now is answered by a sentence of, say, more than say 10 words, it's your mind. An "aha" from the soul is going to be shorter than that. It doesn't need to be lengthy because it's not processed by the mind. It's an energetic truth expressed briefly in order to really sink in. If what is true now starts to have a lengthy explanation, suspect that the mind is encroaching on the soul's turf and ask the mind to shut up.

When used with consistency and consciousness, what is true now can be used to uncover unconscious coping mechanisms and lies that you tell yourself.

◆◆◆

Veronica writes:
Another tool to keep very close to you. I use this one a lot to help sort out when I am acting from my current preferences and when I am acting habitually or out of patterns from the past.

◆◆◆

I like "What is true now." I find the greatest challenge is being aware when the chatter-y monkey-mind starts with its unsuspectingly clever maneuvering to make me feel uncomfortable or irritated or going around and around on the same conversation. Old news, stuff that is past its expiry date, as they say. When I realize it, I immediately go to "What is true now." What is usually "true now" is that I was enjoying whatever I was doing before the sneaky bits got into my conscious thoughts. It seems never-ending.

—*Rosie*

Who answers the door? The current version of you

A PRACTICAL EXAMPLE:
The ex-boyfriend is banging on the front door, you go to answer it but you don't want to talk to him—ask yourself, "Who answers the door?"

Does the four-year-old who's looking for her daddy's approval answer the door? Does the 20-year-old who just wants a boyfriend because she doesn't want to be alone answer the door? Does the 40-year-old who doesn't want to be divorced answer the door? Or does the you of the now that knows that guy shouldn't be in your life answer the door? Who answers the door? You decide that.

This tool is empowering because you say, "OK, I'm not bringing the 4-, 20-, or 40-year-old into this. The current version of me knows that I no longer want this guy in my life. The current version of me can say, 'No'." The four-year-old probably wouldn't be able to say no because the four-year-old's still looking for daddy to make it right, and the 20-year-old still feels like she did something wrong, so she's going to have a hard time saying no, the 40-year-old's feeling like he might be her last chance at love, so she's not turning him away.

But in the moment where you bring your high-vibrational self together and you look at that person and you say, "In this moment, with who I am right now, this situation is not OK, and you need to leave. Off you go. The door's getting locked behind you." And then you turn the ringer off on the phone and you just sit with the fact that you actually made a decision based on who you are today. That's where you give yourself the gift of being who you are today and living your life from who you are today, rather than allowing all baggage from the past or projecting into the future.

USING THIS TOOL WITH FAMILY MEMBERS:
A lot of times, when you're working with biological relatives, the stuff that you're learning about is the stuff from when you were five. However, now you're 40 and you're still doing your five-year-old shit, often from a five-year-old's perspective. Work on the issue when you're 40 as a forty-year-old, rather than, "I'm 40 but I'm acting like I'm five, which I've been doing for 35 years with my mom." This gives you a better chance of success, or a different chance of success, of actually learning and growing and becoming more of who you are.

Yes, you can say, "There's something for me to learn here, but my God, me as a 40-year-old trying to act like an eight-year-old with my mom who is now 70, is not working." It's not working and you have the right to say, "I want to learn this some other way."

This is loving yourself, giving yourself permission to set boundaries across your life. Set the boundaries you need to set in order to give yourself the best chance at learning what it is you desire to learn.

◆◆◆

Veronica writes:
I remember so clearly the first time Eloheim talked about this tool. I was channeling in a living room facing the front door, so it was very visceral imagining the ex-boyfriend on the other side. I have used this tool time and time again in almost every sort of situation. Definitely one of my favorites.

◆◆◆

I have used this tool, especially with my birth family members, where it was easy to slip into being a 10-year-old again. I no longer do that. I now respond and create from the person I am in the moment.

    —Randy Sue

Terms

5D
Shorthand term for expressing the soul experiencing the human form with a consciousness-based operating system. 5D is the experience of Homo spiritus, where the body is lived from an ensouled perspective.

ABUNDANCE
Abundance and "your abundant nature" are terms to describe the energetics reflecting the dynamic scope of possibility offered at this time, a concept meant to reflect the infinite possibilities (of all types) that exist in your physical world.

Our favorite way to illustrate the concept of true abundance is to have people look at how much nature surrounds them, for example: grass, trees, air, sky, and clouds. When one finds oneself lacking abundance, it is important to remember that abundance always exists in nature, and that is the place to start. You can also look at people smiling, hair on people's heads, or how many people have shoes. The point is to find a way to look into the world and see that there is much abundance.

The term abundance has also been corrupted to mean great sums of money or hoarding. Abundance, as an expanded definition, requires that one breaks the cycle or releases the belief that abundance only reflects how much money one has or how many houses one

owns, to instead reflect any place where there is plenty or plentiful-
ness. One simply needs to shift one's perspective about what plenty
or abundance is.

AHA

A moment of clarity and insight that comes from accessing the
soul's perspective; contrast this with the repetitive hamster-wheel-
mind habit of thinking.

Ahas are commonly experienced while in the shower or doing
other tasks that don't require full attention. The path of ascension
and the choice for consciousness facilitate experiencing a steady
stream of ahas.

AKASHIC RECORD

The galactic Internet.

A term that reflects the totality of: all of the lifetimes of those who
have experienced Earth, all of the time that one has spent between
lifetimes, all of the time spent in other incarnational opportunities,
and all the time spent as a soul doing whatever the soul wanted to
do. Think of a giant library where you each have your own section
or file containing everything that has ever been recorded regarding
what you've done, how you've lived, and what you've encountered.
This isn't kept in anything that would resemble a library but it is
helpful to think of it in this way conceptually.

Your Akashic Record is a reservoir of information that makes up
the body of your soul. The energy that reflects that reservoir of
information is what would be correlated to the physicality of the
soul, if the soul had physicality.

When you are not in body and encounter another soul, your section of the Akashic Records is the information presented to the
other soul. Your Akashic Record is the information that your soul
presents to other souls at first glance.

ALTERNATE EXPRESSIONS

Your "past and future" lives. Since time is not linear, these so-called
"past and future" lives are all happening simultaneously; therefore
your "other" lives can be referred to as alternate expressions of you.

AMNESIA

The term we use to describe the "clean slate" of forgetfulness that a human experiences to facilitate living in physical form. It is a necessary state of being to incarnate into the physical body. Amnesia allows you to focus on the present moment in the present lifetime, without distractions from other lifetimes.

If you did not have amnesia about previous Earth experiences and incarnations it would be virtually impossible to stay in the moment because you'd be too busy wanting to go finish, redo, or undo things that have happened in alternate expressions.

ASCENSION

Ascension is a gradual, albeit drastic, transformation from a fear-based operating system into a consciousness-based operating system. Ascension requires evolution in the physical form and a radical shift in the way you respond to the biological messages the body offers.

Ascension is the term assigned to the energetic of the evolutionary leap into Homo spiritus. The Homo spiritus energetic allows for a life to be lived from the soul's perspective, and for a transformed way of interacting with physical matter.

Ascension does not mean you're leaving the body or the planet. Ascension means you're experiencing being in-body on Earth in a brand-new way that is a higher-vibrational, conscious way of living from your soul's perspective in which a spiritual partnership is formed between the soul, physical form, and personality self.

AURA

A way of describing the energy field that surrounds objects, people, animals, and even places. Another way of describing the emanation of individuality; the emanation of the truth of you.

A person's aura is most easily perceivable 4-8 feet from the body; however, auras extend out infinitely.

BAGGAGE

The past, future, cultural pressures, DNA pressures, habits, triggers, and other static that get in the way of you experiencing the moment.

BOUNDARIES

Using your ability as a creator while living in a free-will zone to choose what you are interested in experiencing; directing the incarnation.

BOUNDARIES WITH CONSEQUENCES

In order to leave fear, victimhood, and low-vibrational states behind, you set boundaries in the moment—boundaries with consequences. Boundaries without consequences are just hot air coming out of your mouth. For example, you might say, "You can't speak to me that way," and then the person speaks to you that way. If you don't then act (enact the consequences), all you're doing is blowing hot air. So, boundaries should have consequences attached for the person you're setting the boundary with: "This is what's acceptable in my life and if that doesn't work for you, then you're not in my life."

Is it hard to say to someone, "I'm setting a boundary with you and there are consequences attached"? Of course it is. Is it hard to continue the relationship without boundaries and feel like a victim all the time? We think that's harder.

BUT AND BECAUSE

We use "but and because" as a red flag to alert you that you may be slipping into victim mentality. If you find yourself using those words, you may be leaving the realm of "I created it" and entering into the position of "it was done to me." Listen to conversation around you and begin to notice how frequently you hear "because this" and "but that."

At times, you may feel like you need to include a "but" or a "because" to feel like you have conveyed your entire story. That may be the case. We are not saying that you should remove them from your language completely. We are suggesting that you become conscious of how you use "but" and "because." We believe it will help uncover places where you are habituating to victimhood.

An example from a conversation about income streams:
You said, "Yeah, I have 35 different ways money comes to me, *but* I still can't pay my bills." Instead say, "I have 35 ways money comes to me. Period."

"But and because" take away your high-vibrational state, they lower your energetic, make it more difficult to reach insight from your soul, and cause you to slip back into thinking, thinking, thinking. Remember, if thinking could have solved it, it would've solved it long ago, because you sure have thought about it enough. We aren't looking to think more, we are seeking insight.

An example from a conversation about trying new things:
You are tempted to say: "Oh, but I couldn't; oh, but I don't; oh, but that's silly; oh, but, oh, but." Right? It does not serve you to "but-and-because" away a fascination. A fascination is present for a reason. The exploration of the fascination is the gift, the gift you give yourself. What exactly do you think your soul's perspective is going to feel like? Souls are very curious. They want to learn and grow and do new things. Is it surprising that the soul's perspective comes in as fascination and curiosity?

CERTAINTY
When you are operating from the fear-based operating system, change feels extremely risky. The survival instinct is constantly pressuring you to stay the same, because "the same" has kept you alive. Any changes to "the same" require certainty about the outcome in order to quiet the fears the survival instin   ct produces. As certainty is a fallacy—you can't be truly certain of anything in the diverse, vast world you find yourself in—you find yourself in a no-win situation: Change requires certainty, certainty is unattainable, and paralysis (fear) is the result.

Evolving your relationship to the survival instinct and certainty is a major aspect of the ascension process.

CHANGE
The recognition of an altered condition in the incarnation, which, if processed habitually, often triggers fear. When processed

consciously, change becomes the mechanism for growth.

CHANNEL

An incarnated soul experiencing the human form that allows non-physical guides to communicate through him or her in order to present helpful information in a palatable form. If out-of-body or non-corporal guides showed up as a burning bush, beam of light, or in a light body of some fashion, they would be far more likely to create fear than comfort. Channeling and channels allow a more human-to-human type of transmission of information, commonly less triggering than other types of transmissions.

CHANNELED MESSAGE

Information that comes through a channel from guides that are not in physical form, but have perspective on the physical journey or the human experiment.

CONSCIOUS/CONSCIOUSNESS

Knowing why you do what you do. Choosing your reactions. Not being driven by habit. Experiencing the world as a creator rather than as a victim.

The world, as you experience it, has been programmed through habits, fears, and your biology. Through attention (consciousness), you can live the bigger picture that includes your personality's paradigm shifting and the embracing of your soul's perspective, as well.

CONSCIOUSNESS-BASED OPERATING SYSTEM (CBOS)

The consciousness-based operating system is the 5D or Homo spiritus way of experiencing the world that allows for conscious interactions with experiences rather than fear-based, habitually driven interaction with experiences.

CREATING YOUR REALITY

"Create your own reality" is one of those terms that's overused and under-understood. Creating your reality is often believed to be a way to *control* your reality. It is thought to be a path to certainty and safety. Creating your reality is actually an outcome of your vibrational self, your vibrational nature, your emanation of a higher-vibrational choice.

Creating your reality works very much like a fountain. The fountain shoots up the water and it sprays out all over the place. No one knows where every drop's going to land. Who would want to? It would be tedious in the extreme. The uncertainty creates the beauty.

Similarly, creating your reality isn't about the outcome (where the drops land), it is about the experience (the beauty of the water in the air.)

In our fountain example, the water represents the truth of you (your soul's perspective and your personality), the water pressure represents your free-will choices and the fountain mechanism represents your preferences and boundaries.

Creating your reality starts with setting boundaries in association with your preferences. You then align your free-will to choose conscious reactions to your experiences (which often has the result of clearing static), and then you and your soul emanate together.

You initiate your creation, you choose how you react to your creation, and you remain open to insight from your soul.

CREATOR, THE
If you believe that this world is created, then there must be a Creator. Therefore, the Creator is the one who created all. It helps to recognize that the Creator is not conceivable in its entirety while experiencing duality because of the inherent limitations of the human mind and the infinite scope of the Creator. However, the Creator can be sensed through insight from your soul and through experiencing creation.

CREATOR/CREATORSHIP
As a creator, you are aware that you are in a free-will zone and that you have the ability to choose your reactions to your experiences. When creations seem to be in opposition to what you "want," creators recognize that there are levels of creation and that everything is happening *for* me, rather than falling into victimhood.

CULTURAL PRESSURES
Cultural pressures include: family beliefs, societal norms, and cus-

toms. Often, cultural pressures present as, "It's what everyone else is doing" and are used to justify forgoing transformation.

Habits and DNA pressures combine with cultural pressures to make a potent combination for habitual response to triggers.

DENSITY

Experiencing the free-will zone in a body. Souls do not have physical form in the same way humans do. Incarnating on Earth provides for the unique experience of density, duality, and free will.

DNA PRESSURES

Your DNA is the blueprint for your body. You and your soul collaborated to create the unique incarnation you are experiencing.

We use the term "DNA pressures" to refer to the interaction habits and consciousness have with your physicality.

As an example: Tall people habitually put things on high shelves while shorter people will habitually put things on lower shelves. Both are examples of people acting based on DNA (and convenience).

DNA pressures combine with cultural pressures to make a potent combination for habitual response to triggers.

DUALITY

The idea that there are only two options, typically experienced as either, "what I think is right and what I think is wrong," or "what they think is right and what they think is wrong." A very limited way to experience Earth and the human form. The fear-based operating system loves duality because it gives a false sense of certainty. (I am RIGHT). The consciousness-based operating system leaves duality behind as it explores the truth of, "Everything that happens, happens for me and is teaching me something."

EARTH

The planet Earth is designated as a free-will zone and was developed to provide opportunities for incarnating souls to experience density and duality. Earth, at this time, is engaged in an ascension process and will reflect a changed environment for ascended beings to explore. What that changed environment will actually look like is unknown, and highly anticipated for that very reason.

ELOHEIM

We, the Eloheim, are a collaboration of souls presenting with a singular voice, channeled through the body of Veronica Torres with her explicit approval, willingness, and allowance. It is our great privilege to offer our support to you at this very exciting time on Earth to facilitate the transformation of Homo sapiens to Homo spiritus; moving from the fear-based operating system to the consciousness-based operating system. It is a grand experiment that many beings in the universe are watching with great interest, awe, and fascination.

EMANATING (THE TRUTH OF YOU)

As you live consciously, you emanate consciousness into your world. Your job is just to contribute, your job is not to try to dictate or control where your contribution to high-vibrational living ends up. It's not your business where it goes or how it shows up in the world.

ENERGETICS

The way that souls communicate through nonverbal knowing. Because your physical forms cannot yet communicate on the level that souls do, nonverbal knowing or "energetics" need to be translated into your language to facilitate understanding and communication.

Since it is always less accurate to use language than it is to communicate energetically, it is our hope and desire that your progress will eventually include the ability to communicate energetically without the need for language.

Energetic communication is happening all the time. Living consciously means that you are emanating a conscious energetic. It really does matter how you handle triggers and other upsets. Not just because it determines how you will experience the triggers, but it also determines how your emanation will go out to others. When we work with you, we are reading your energetics far more than we are listening to your words. Your energetics often show us visuals, which we can use to facilitate deeper understanding of the situations you are experiencing.

ENSOULMENT

The process by which soul energy is more deeply experienced by the personality incarnated in the physical form as the perspective is shifted from one of a survival instinct to a soul's perspective—from a fear-based operating system to a consciousness-based operating system.

Ensoulment, or living from the soul's perspective, is a collaboration between the personality self (you incarnate as a human) and your soul's wisdom. Don't misunderstand this to be that your soul "takes you over." This is not the case.

As an example, let's say you take a calculus class. The you at the end of the class hasn't 'taken over' the you from the beginning of the class. You have become a being that has the additional experience of the wisdom you gained in your studies.

Ensoulment is you realizing the wisdom and insight your soul already has; the completeness of you.

FEAR

Fear is a biological reaction to change or the idea of change that typically creates the "fight or flight" response in the body, which is an adrenaline-based response to, "What do I do next?" Typically, the answer is that you run habit.

Consciously experiencing fear presents opportunities for extreme growth because it gives you the opportunity to break habitual patterns—to experience the moment rather than experiencing habit, which often involves projection of the future or bringing a memory of the past into the moment.

Fear can also be defined as the biological component of duality. It is the biological response to the belief in duality that is enacted regardless of which side of duality you're on. If you're on the side of duality that says, "This is wrong," then there's fear for survival. If you're on the side that says, "This is right," there's fear that it won't continue. Fear and the survival instinct work together to keep you small.

FEAR-BASED

Actions based on fear rather than conscious choice, a habitual, unconscious mentality (operating system) based on fear.

FEAR-BASED OPERATING SYSTEM (FBOS)

You are a fear-based being. It is not something you can argue. It is a fact. Period. Full stop. End of sentence. You cannot argue with the fact that you are a fear-based being because you have been built to operate from fear in order to continue surviving. You've been built to startle at loud noises. You've been built to have the fight-or-flight response trigger in you. You've been built to be wary and aware of your surroundings. All of this can be summarized or reduced to fear. There is no need to be ashamed of admitting the fears that you find yourself experiencing because it is a core aspect of being human. You were brought into this incarnation running the fear-based operating system, meaning you're constantly experiencing the world based on fear. The survival instinct is continuously asking you to be wary. The survival instinct is continuously trying to keep you small and it has extreme measures it can go to in order to keep you from sticking your neck out, from standing out in the crowd, from being noticed. The survival instinct flares up in you and requires your habitual responses to stimulus and triggers.

As consciousness is applied to the fear-based operating system, and as you break out of habitual response patterns, you're able to experience what is going on in your life from a new perspective and shift into a consciousness-based operating system.

FREE WILL

Free will is the opportunity to be in amnesia about the truth of you: the truth of your infinite, immortal nature.

Free will allows you to experience Earth as YOU see fit. No one can interfere with your chosen experience—not your soul, and not even The Creator.

Note, we said your chosen experience. You choose how you experience everything. Your free will gives you this ability. Now, we are not saying that everything that happens in your life feels like something you have chosen on a personality level; however, your chosen reaction to everything that happens in your life is within your purview.

Free will gives you the option to break out of the fear-based operating system, to break habits, exercise change and choose consciousness.

FREE-WILL ZONE

An experiment that was initiated by The Eloheim after being invited by The Creator to come up with something new for souls to experience. It is an opportunity for souls to incarnate in a completely amnesic state and live a lifetime through their own direction, without influence from external forces, to grow as a soul. The free-will zone is inclusive of the solar system that holds Earth.

GROWTH

Consciousness infusing the incarnation, resulting in transformation.

GUIDES

A generic or general term used for beings that are not currently in physical form that are available to assist those who are in physical form, through a variety of means—through channels, through coincidence, through synchronicities, through dreams, and many other ways.

HABIT/HABITUAL RESPONSE

Habit is tied into the fear of getting dead and the survival instinct. Since the body is programmed to stay alive, it will say, "Well, this hasn't killed me yet, so let's continue." Change makes the body feel like there's a potential to get killed. Change means new factors to manage, new things to deal with, and new situations to juggle. It is easier on the body if it already knows the threats that are involved in your day-to-day life and has already established that none of them are threatening enough to get you dead. The body is going to want to keep repeating that pattern. If you know that a food is poisonous to you, you don't eat it again—making that a healthy habit. But the survival instinct, as translated into 21st-century Earth, ends up looking like, "I can't quit this job that I hate because I'm too afraid of getting dead. I'm too engrained in this habit to try something else."

HAMSTER-WHEEL THINKING

The habitual mind repetitiously trying to think its way out of "problems." Repetitious thinking about past and/or future experiences misses the experience of the moment.

HIGH-VIBRATIONAL

High-vibrational refers to actions, thoughts, ideas, and relationships which are based on consciousness and conscious choices. It is not a judgmental term; rather it is descriptive of the fact that your body is actually vibrating at a different rate than it did before you infused consciousness into your life.

Your soul vibrates at a very high rate. Raising your vibration by living consciously is a very important step in living from your soul's perspective and walking the path of ascension.

HOARDING

One of the most low-vibrational states you experience. "I'm going to look out for me and I don't care what happens to other people." Hoarders are constantly in lack and looking for how they can get more. They are obsessed by the question, "How can I get what I don't have?" They never feel like they have enough of what they need.

HOMO SPIRITUS

A name for a state of being that is possible when you live in collaboration with your soul incorporating your soul's perspective; a transformed, expanded experience of the physical form and a shifted paradigm of how one is on Earth.

Living from the consciousness-based operating system, pursuing the path of ascension.

INSIGHT

Information received directly from your soul.

The challenge when explaining the word "insight" is that it is a process that uses the brain but must not be confused with "thinking."

There are a few characteristics that illuminate the differences between the two: the mind is limited and will often present limiting messages. The mind's messages are repetitive and often negative. Insight will present ideas and options you've never considered before, which are always positive and constructive in their nature. Insight will never demean you; it will never be negative and it will always be supportive of your growth and transformation.

KARMA

The word "karma" had a strong definition coming out of Eastern religious beliefs. When it came to the West, the term became somewhat bastardized to mean, "If you're not good, something bad is going to happen to you."

Karma had a big duality perspective in it but if you take the duality out of it, it becomes, "Everything teaches me," instead of, "I'm waiting to get punished for any mistakes or slip-ups I make."

LEARNING

As an incarnate soul, the processes that you go through in order to have the growth you desire are called "learning." The journey is a journey of change, shifts, transformation, and ascension, which is all brought into the physical system through the process of internal and external transformation, a reflection of all of the learning that has occurred.

LIGHT WORKER

A soul incarnating at this time with the specific desire to grow spiritually and live consciously. A person walking the path of ascension. A Homo sapiens desiring to live as Homo spiritus.

LOW-VIBRATIONAL

A state of being that comes from living in the fear-based operating system, not looking for conscious understanding or an experience of the dynamics being presented to you. Living habitually rather than opening to new experience.

It is not a judgmental term; rather, it is descriptive of the fact that your body is actually vibrating at a different rate than it would if you infused consciousness into your life.

Your soul vibrates at a very high rate. It is difficult to connect to your soul's energy when living a low-vibrational life.

MIND

The mind's thoughts and insight are both processed by the brain. The mind is only capable of taking the spiritual journey so far. At some point, the mind's ability to manage the spiritual journey comes to a standstill. Without the infusion of insight from the soul, the journey will stagnate. When you act, react, and create only from your mind, you're cutting yourself off from the vast resources of your soul and the Akashic Records. In this context, it's easy to see that allowing the mind to run the incarnation is limiting.

PEACE

Peace is the experience of you being non-disturbable. It is the idea that no matter what's going on you know what your center is. You know the truth of you and you don't resist it. You can have peace even with things you hate about yourself if you don't resist the truth of you being present. Peace is: "No matter what's going on, I'm still me. No matter who's triggering me, I'm still me."

PERSONALITY

The aspect of the incarnate human that has a name, that has preferences, that has a history, that has a future, that has relationships. It's the aspect of you that's currently under development.

The power of the personality is that it wields free will. Therefore, the personality actually is completely in charge of the incarnation by controlling whether or not consciousness is employed, deciding how to react to situations, and deciding whether or not to pursue ascension.

PREFERENCES/JUDGMENTS

Judgment is not the same as preference. Judgment is the belief that you have to have a position against something in order to have a position preferring something. So, all of a sudden the choice between chocolate and vanilla must become, "Chocolate is a good flavor and vanilla is a bad flavor, so I am going with chocolate because that's the good flavor,instead of just saying, "I have a preference for chocolate."

You're an immortal, infinite soul that chooses to have every experience you can manage. If you set out a lot of judgments and you start saying that vanilla's wrong, then when it comes around time to experience vanilla you have to deal with the baggage of already assigning it as wrong. It's always nice to not put extra baggage on things that you'll probably get around to wanting to experience someday. I's also quite helpful to limit the amount of baggage (static) about anything you are experiencing.

Most of the time, we see that you had to make one thing wrong—sometimes VERY wrong—in order to set a preference because you weren't feeling strong enough to just say "No" is a complete sentence.

When you are new to boundaries and preferences you will sometimes believe that you have to get really worked up in order to use them. Actually, when you discover "What is true now?," you can set boundaries and state preferences from a very calm place.

Keep in mind that there is a damned good reason for having a preference, which is: You're a soul experiencing the physical form in a free-will zone. So, if you don't have some preferences, what the heck is the point of being here in the first place? Not very much that we can see. Having preferences is the one of the main events!

Someone once said to us, "Well, if we are infinite and immortal, aren't we going to do everything?" And we said yes, but you do them in an order. There's an order to it. In a linear sense, there's an order to it. Where today you decided to eat chocolate, tomorrow you're going to decide to eat vanilla. So, even if you're immortal and infinite, you're still deciding right now to be here instead of being someplace else. Preference. Choice. Free will. You don't need to have something be wrong in order to have something else be what you want to do.

Coming from judgment is low-vibrational. It takes a lot of energy to stay invested in a judgment. It can be difficult to change your mind because you are so invested energetically in the judgment. Sometimes your identity can even be wrapped up in a judgment, which makes it that much harder to change. Judgments don't serve you, on so many levels.

SAFETY

The idea that you can control outcomes. Safety is sought by looking for certainty. Certainty is a fallacy—it can never be achieved. Everything has some degree of uncertainty in it. The survival instinct constantly pushes you to seek safety; the fear-based operating system gives you no way to get there. The ascension journey helps you learn that the only sense of true safety comes from a deep connection to your soul and moving moment to moment through clarity.

SHADOW

The aspects of yourself that you don't want anybody else to know about; the things that you are ashamed of and deny, and repress; places where you don't love yourself yet, parts of you that you reject as unacceptable, wrong, bad, or even evil; aspects of your life you feel are socially unacceptable yet still true; honest experiences that you have had that you didn't handle with consciousness; shame: these from your shadow.

We see your shadow aspects as dark holes or gray areas in your energy body that make you look a bit like Swiss cheese.

Our desire is to help you love all parts of yourself, which allows you to live from the soul's perspective as a Homo spiritus being.

SOUL

The infinite, immortal nature of your true self, including the collection of every lifetime you've had on Earth, the time between lifetimes, every lifetime you've had in other incarnational opportunities, and all other experiences.

The soul is a vast reservoir of experience and an eternally curious being.

Animating a human body does not require the entirety of your soul. There is no way you can stuff an entire soul into a human body. But there's a percentage of your soul that has been allocated to be experience-able in this lifetime.

SOUL'S PERSPECTIVE

The wisdom of your soul incorporated into your experience of being human. It's the insight available to you when you live from the consciousness-based operating system.

From the soul's perspective, there is no judgment, no duality, no fear about life in the physical form. Everything is fascinating.

Your soul knows this is all just a journey in learning. There's no right, there's no wrong, there's no good, there's no bad. It's a journey in learning, exploration, experience. It's not the destination—it's the journey.

SPIRITUALITY

Functioning from more than just the survival instinct. Awareness of and openness to experiences outside of those that are "provable" or "repeatable." Knowledge that you are more than just this human form.

SPIRITUAL GROWTH

Another term for transformation and learning, indicating that your learning is not based on your mind or habits but on consciousness-based transformation.

STATIC

Unconscious reactions and thoughts; coping mechanisms, masks, lies, baggage, dishonesty, hiding from your authentic expression or the completeness of you; anything that interrupts your ability to stay in the authentic truth of the moment. The mind, the survival instinct, the body, and fear all generate static to keep you small.

Static includes all the reasons you have sold yourself on which you use to avoid presenting the truth of you to the world. It will crop up more intensely as you start to recognize the greatness and the vastness of your true self.

Living consciously is the path to clearing static.

SUFFERING

Suffering occurs when you experience the world from a victim mentality—not believing you are a creator and instead living in limitation and habit.

You've all suffered, and you have the choice in the suffering to experience it as learning. No matter what is occurring, there's always that choice. Change happens. What is, is. Let's look at it from a new perspective. Do you want to climb out of this new experience with something learned from it, or do you want to wallow in what happened to you, in victimhood?

SURVIVAL INSTINCT

A body-based dynamic that puts the continuation of life at the top of the list of importance. The survival instinct serves you deeply by continuing life even when physical, mental, or emotional experiences lead you to feeling as though you want your life to end.

There had to be a survival instinct put into the system because duality is so different from your experience of being a soul that it would be very tempting to "drop one toe into this water" and then run away. The body's innate survival instinct keeps you in the incarnation long enough to be able to make conscious choices about the experience.

In order to live a conscious life, one must transform one's relationship to the survival instinct. Consciousness asks you to make steps toward change that the survival instinct will be resistant to embrace because to the body, any change feels like potential death and therefore, should be avoided at all costs.

The survival instinct is one of your greatest treasures as well as one of the most challenging places to transform with consciousness because it's so deeply based in the body, and based in unconscious processing. When you are able to consciously modify the way the survival instinct works in the incarnation, you open yourself up to a deep and profound way of re-experiencing how it is to be human. This is one of the major steps in living as Homo spiritus, as an ascended being.

THINKING

The process by which the brain exerts control over the incarnation.

The survival instinct is often the driving force behind thinking. Thinking is often employed to avoid experiencing change, transformation, or growth. In the spiritual journey, transforming your thought process with consciousness to choose insight from your soul rather than small-mind thinking is one of the major steps to becoming an ascended being.

The brain is the thinking organ. The mind is the thought process. Insight, which comes from your soul, can feel like thinking, however, the content will clarify if you are thinking or receiving insight.

TOOLS
Techniques used to interrupt the unconscious running of habit by using consciousness to shift out of a fear-based operating system into the consciousness-based operating system. See the table of contents for a list of tools included in this book.

TRANSFORMATION
A term describing change, especially change along the ascension process.

TRIGGERS
Triggers are stimuli that the personality experiences which bring up opportunities to explore unhealed parts of the personality self.

UNCONSCIOUS
Acting from the fear-based operating system without the intervention of consciousness; running habit.

VIBRATION
LOW VIBRATION: A state of being that comes from living from the fear-based operating system, not looking for conscious understanding or experience of the dynamics being presented to you. Living habitually rather than opening to new experience.

It is not a judgmental term, rather it is descriptive of the fact that your body is actually vibrating at a different rate than it would if you infused consciousness into your life.

Your soul vibrates at a very high rate. It is difficult to connect to your soul's energy when living a low-vibrational life.

HIGH-VIBRATION: A description of actions, thoughts, ideas, and relationships which are based on consciousness and conscious choices. It is not a judgmental term, rather it is descriptive of the fact that your body is actually vibrating at a different rate than it did before you infused consciousness into your life.

Your soul vibrates at a very high rate. Raising your vibration by living consciously is a very important step in living from your soul's perspective and walking the path of ascension.

VICTIM/VICTIMHOOD

The mistaken perspective that things happen to you that you are at the whim of any other creature, being, person, or eventuality that you experience while on Earth. Running the fear-based operating system. It is a perspective that is very easy to assume because you incarnate with amnesia, making it difficult for you to remember your infinite nature, or the fact that you planned to be here and have the experiences you are having.

When events trigger you or you have experiences that you deem negative, your reaction is, "Why did this happen to me?" which is a victim's perspective. With a conscious journey and a conscious life, you're able to start seeing the world as the creator that you are, and start asking, "Why is this happening *for* me?" and realizing that "Everything teaches me something."

YOUR INTERNAL WORLD CREATES YOUR EXTERNAL JOURNEY

Your internal world is the creation point for the external expression of your life. Not the other way around. Your internal process is projected on the movie screen of your external life where it all plays out. This allows you to learn and grow from the experience of observing your internal life projected (externalized).

Your internal world is a series of choices that you've made, even if the choice was to default to a habitual pattern, to default to a culturally driven pattern, to default to the childhood pattern. Those are still choices.

Remember, it can't happen in your external world unless it's true in your internal world. When experiences arise, ask, "What are you showing me about me? What are you telling me about me?" Let the experiences inform you rather than staying with the surface reaction of, "They're just triggering me or challenging me or frustrating me or driving me bananas." Ask instead, "What are you showing me about me?"

You can't dictate how people react to you, necessarily, but you can certainly influence the outcome by loving yourself well and sending that into the world instead of doubt and anguish and anxiety and feeling stepped on and being a victim and all that. If you walk into a room knowing you love yourself and emanating your truth, you're going to have a different experience than if you walk into a room feeling like a victim and a doormat. You will be known and reacted to by the way you love yourself.

Your awareness of your internal world becomes so rich and well-developed, so well-known and mapped by you, that your emanation of the truth of your internal world starts to resemble a fountain that bubbles up and spills over without stopping. It's not something you have to think about or work yourself through or get going. It bubbles up in you and it spills over, just like a fountain does, the fullness of your internal world emanating out into the world. This doesn't involve you acting in the world as much as it involves you experiencing the world from your truth. The truth of you being real.

Appendix

What is channeling?

Channeling is a process where I set my personality aside to allow Eloheim and The Council to use my physical form to convey their teachings.

PLEASE NOTE: This is not possession. It only occurs when I give explicit permission. I can stop it at ANY time.

When I am channeling I feel as though I am standing or sitting behind and to the left of my actual body. I am aware of what is being said as the session unfolds, although I don't always remember everything that is discussed.

Eloheim and The Council specialize in reading the energy of a question, situation, or person. They often experience visual representations of the energy they sense. When this occurs, I see it as a "movie" in my head not unlike what happens when I am dreaming.

I have created a YouTube video with more details about the process. You can watch it by searching YouTube for: "Introduction Eloheim and The Council."

Who are Eloheim and The Council?

On February 11, 1997, I had a reading by a very skilled psychic and channel. During that reading he said that I would become a channel myself. Although I valued much of what he shared, my reaction to that statement was, YEAH, RIGHT!

I was quite familiar with channeling. I found it incredibly valuable. I just didn't see myself doing it!

That all changed when I came to Sonoma. I was invited to a friend's home to do a Lakshmi puja. The chanting left me in a very altered state. When we finished, we sat in a circle on the floor. I told one of the participants I had a message for her and then shared information she found very helpful. At the end of the sharing I said, "We are the Eloheim and we are pleased to have been with you today."

Now, even though I knew what had happened, I was overwhelmed by it and started to cry. It didn't feel bad or wrong, just very intense. It made me feel very conspicuous. I immediately told myself, "That's never going to happen again."

It was some time before it did. Over time, I got more comfortable with the idea of being a channel but I had no idea how to do it! I tried to work with Eloheim on my own once or twice. I even recorded a very useful message about habitual response on November 26, 2000, yet it just wasn't coming together. Almost two years passed without much forward movement.

Finally, a friend and I figured it out. What was needed was a second person to ask the questions and help me with the logistics of the whole thing.

In the very beginning while channeling, I had to raise my right hand in order to receive the energies (boy, am I glad that I don't have to do that any longer). I would get very thirsty, but I wasn't able to hold a glass (I still have a bunch of straws in a drawer from those days). I had a TON of insecurity about "Am I making this up?" and "Is this real?" and "Am I doing it right?" I needed a lot of reassurance just to stick with it. I would get very sleepy afterward and sometimes needed help just getting around. I had to eat a lot of protein to keep my energy level up.

Details, details, details. All of which felt completely unmanageable to me alone, but became possible once I had help.

After about one month, Eloheim told us that this wasn't just for the two of us and to get a group together. That was September 2002, when we began our weekly Eloheim sessions. We still hold meetings every Wednesday night and one Sunday per month. You can join us live or tune into our webcasts. For more information, please visit: eloheim.com/web-casts.

I had never heard the term Eloheim until they introduced themselves that way. Someone then told me it was one of the names of God. I looked it up on the Internet and found that to be true. It is important to note that although it is common to see the spelling Elohim, I was guided to use the spelling Eloheim.

Eloheim has made it clear that just as not everyone named John is the same, to not assume that all entities using the name Eloheim or Elohim are the same. The material they present with me is internally consistent and can be taken as a whole.

Eloheim is a group entity that presents with one voice. That one voice feels like a male energy. We refer to the Eloheim as "he" or "they."

They refer to themselves as "we."

Starting on June 10, 2009, I began channeling the rest of The Council. Here are the dates of their first appearances:

The Visionaries - 06/10/2009

The Guardians - 12/02/2009

The Girls - 01/06/2010

The Matriarch - 02/03/2010

The Warrior - 03/17/2010

Fred - 06/30/2010

For more information about Eloheim and The Council, please visit: eloheim.com/who-is-eloheim

What is it like to channel Eloheim and The Council?

Eloheim:
I have been channeling Eloheim since 2002. They are very easy to channel. I've channeled them while riding in a car, in a room full of playing puppies, in a haunted winery, on the radio, during an earthquake (briefly), and in all sorts of other places. They are the only Council member who I channel with eyes open. Perhaps someday other Council members will be ready for eyes open, but at this time they are all still getting used to interacting with the body and the additional stimulus of eyes open would be too much—for me and for them.

Visionaries (first channeled on 06/10/2009):
The Visionaries were the first to join Eloheim on the Council. After seven years of working with Eloheim, it was strange to imagine channeling another group. Little did I know it was just the beginning! Here are some of my comments from the first time I channeled the Visionaries:

They sat right on the edge of the chair. They are even louder than Eloheim. They use language differently and have a different cadence to their speech. I found my jaw moving in strange ways to accommodate this.

Nowadays, the Visionaries continue to be intense, but I am much more comfortable with their energy. I frequently wonder how they can say so many words in such a short period of time. They are the most rigid of the Council members and often seem to have their entire talk planned out ahead of time. To watch video from their first appearance, please visit this page on my website: http://eloheim.com/1064/eloheim-the-visionaries/.

Guardians (first channeled on 12/02/2009):
When the Guardians first came in, they had a very hard time talking. However, they sure could MOVE energy. They continue to focus on working energetically with us although they can talk easily now. A lot of what I experience when channeling the Guardians is sensing the energy they are picking up in the room. There are sometimes visuals associated with the energy, but it is more often a sense of knowing rather than seeing.

Watch their first video on this page: http://eloheim.com/1792/eloheim-3rd-and-4th-chakras-emotions-guardians-and-visionaries/.

The Girls (first channeled on 01/06/2010):
I just found this quote from my first blog posting about the Girls, "The Girls immediately sat back in the chair, got comfortable, crossed my legs, and settled in for a chat." That pretty much sums it up. They come in and chat with us. They are very comfortable with the body and very easy to channel. They have a light energy which is quite fun for me to experience. Watch their first video on this page: http://eloheim.com/2000/eloheim-10610/.

The Matriarch (first channeled on 02/03/2010):
I don't really remember much from the first time I channeled the Matriarch. Mostly I remember being sort of overwhelmed by the idea that we were *still* adding new groups to the channeling. I wasn't all that keen about the idea. However, the Matriarch is amazing to channel. Sometimes my heart opens so much that it feels like the entire room is inside of me. I feel loved and embraced by her. I am so happy she closes out our meetings. It is a wonderful energy to conclude the meeting with. You can watch her first appearance here: http://eloheim.com/2197/eloheim-audio-from-2-3-10-meeting/.

The Warrior (first channeled on 03/17/2010):
The Warrior was really hard to channel the first time. It took
me six days to feel like myself again. I couldn't watch the
video or listen to the audio without their energy coming back
into my body and I just couldn't manage it. When they first
came in, it felt like my entire body grew by two inches and
then snapped back to its normal size. I was sore from head
to toe the next morning. It was a strange time. Now, I have
a total crush on the Warrior. I don't have a "favorite"—really
I don't—but it's tempting! I get a bonus when I channel the
Warrior. It is as though I am watching a movie when they tell
their stories. My eyes are closed, but I see a complete, full-color
movie in my head. I don't get anything like that from any of
the other Council members. It's really cool. Here is video from
the Warrior's second appearance: http://eloheim.com/2529/
eloheim-this-is-a-choice-the-warrior-and-more-3-24-10/.

Fred (first channeled on 06/30/2010):
Fred is a total trip. I still don't think I "get" him. He carries a
Galactic energy which is really huge, but very non-physical.
Weird…it's weird and hard to explain. He took quite a while to
figure out how to interact with the body. He's getting much better
now. Fred is the opposite of the Visionaries. The Visionaries come
in with a plan, Fred seems to not have a clue what he wants to
talk about until the second he starts talking! People just love Fred
and have powerful reactions to him. He gets more fan mail than
any of the others! I have a suspicion that Fred will end up rock-
ing my world. However, he mostly just confuses me at this point.
You can watch his first video here: http://eloheim.com/3275/
eloheim-and-the-full-council-fred-joins-us-6-30-10/.

Overall, channeling the Council is a very enjoyable experience.
There have been plenty of times when I was practically non-func-
tional the day after a meeting, but that seems to have passed. I
learned that if I eat something really salty—popcorn works
well—after a meeting, I usually feel fine the next day.

About the author

Veronica Torres: is based in Sonoma, CA. She has channeled Eloheim since 2002, both in public and private sessions. Her public channeling sessions are offered five times per month. These sessions are broadcast live on the Internet and archived for on-demand viewing.

Veronica's career history is interesting and varied, with work including: talk radio host, Rock and Roll memorabilia store owner, Network Director of a Holistic Practitioner's Group, Producer of Well Being Expos, and jewelry designer!

Photo credit: nancikerby.com

Contact

Website: eloheim.com

Facebook: facebook.com/eloheim

Twitter: twitter.com/channelers

YouTube: youtube.com/eloheimchannel

Join our live channeling sessions in person or online:
eloheim.com/web-casts

Visit our meeting archives for video and audio recordings of past gatherings, and our entire book catalog:
eloheim.com/cart

Join our mailing list:
tinyurl.com/eloheimlist

Private session with Eloheim:
eloheim.com/meeting-schedule-private-sessions/

Videos:
eloheim.com/eloheim-videos/

Preview other Eloheim books

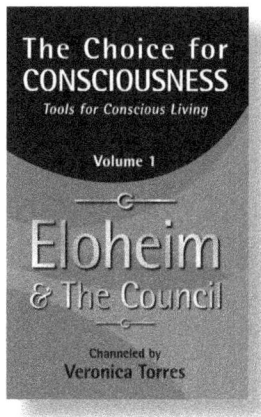

The Choice for Consciousness, Tools for Conscious Living, Vol. 1

Why would you want to make the choice for consciousness? What are tools for conscious living?

Two very important questions.

Here are four more: Are you living in peace? Are you living in joy? Are you living in serenity? Are you living in bliss?

And, the most important question: Are you ready to take bold steps in that direction?

Moving out of a fear-based operating system into a consciousness-based operating system allows you to experience being human in a brand-new way. A way that isn't driven by habit, repetitive thinking, reliving the past, speculating about the future, or being paralyzed by the fear of change.

Consciousness is a way of living that focuses on an authentic experience of the moment, awareness of your truth, and the full comprehension that by choosing your reaction to every one of your experiences, you are creating your reality.

This book contains simple but powerful tools that will help you make the shift from the fear-based operating system (survival) to the consciousness-based operating system (fascination).

These tools can be used throughout your spiritual journey. They require no props, no rituals, no religious beliefs, and can be easily incorporated into your day-to-day activities. In addition, they build on one another and can be used in powerful combinations that will rapidly transform your experience.

The first section introduces 22 tools. The second section defines and clarifies nearly 126 terms and concepts. You can read this volume in any order. It is not a narrative, but a reference book you will likely turn to time and time again.

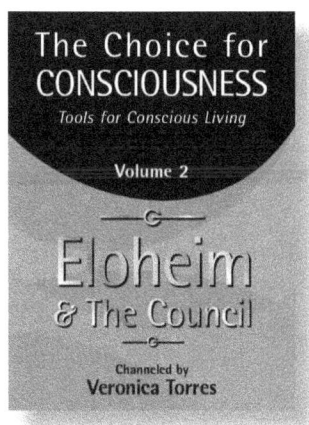

The Choice for Consciousness, Tools for Conscious Living, Vol. 2

Through the act of loving yourself, you give the gift of the truth of you to this world.

The most powerful way you can be in the world is by loving yourself well and then living your life from that place. The question is: how do you do that? How do you love yourself when faced with overwhelming responsibilities, guilt, and feeling like the world is stacked against you?

You love yourself well when you make the choice for consciousness. Consciousness changes the way you view yourself and the way you view your life.

Change is rarely easy; yet staying the same offers no relief from suffering. The choice for consciousness is challenging, but familiar suffering is painful--and it's a pain with no end in sight!

This book provides step-by-step support to help you release victim mentality; drop baggage and unhealthy habits; and discard fear-based living. It will show you how to live as the creator of your life.

This volume contains 16 tools and 126 definitions of terms and concepts to support your journey. The tools can be used in any order and are very powerful when combined with each other.

The fear of change and the habit of staying small collaborate to say, "No, no, no, don't you dare change because that could be dangerous. Who knows what will happen if you change?" That's the moment when you have to take the risk of allowing yourself to walk the truth of you in the world. When you hear the voice that says, "No, no, no, I can't be that big. I can't shine my light that much. I can't emanate the truth of me to these people," that's the point when you need to say instead, "I want healing above all else. I want healing above all else. My desire for healing is stronger than my fear of what will happen if I shine my light, than my fear of how my truth will be received. My desire for healing is stronger than that. Emanation of the truth of me comes first."

The *Choice for Consciousness, Tools for Conscious Living* series offers channeled messages from Eloheim and The Council.

The Council is comprised of seven different groups: The Guardians, The Girls, The Visionaries, The Matriarch, The Eloheim, The Warrior, and Fred. During a channeling session, each of The Council members take turns sharing their teachings. Each Council member has a distinct personality, style of delivery, and focus.

The Council is best known for their multitude of practical tools, which support the journey out of fear-based living into the consciousness-based operating system.

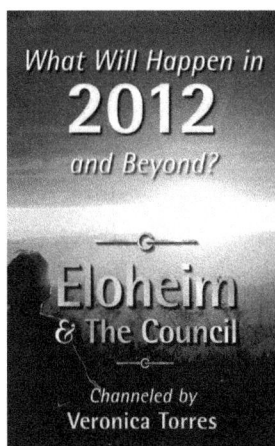

What Will Happen in 2012 and Beyond?

The question, "What will happen in 2012?" is being asked by a great many people. The Mayan calendar ends on December 21, 2012 which has given rise to a considerable amount of speculation about what might happen, including predictions that the world will either end or that we will experience some sort of catastrophic event.

With so much fear and uncertainty surrounding "What will happen in 2012?", we decided to ask Eloheim for their perspective.

In this 57 page book, Eloheim explains how we can use the energies of "2012" for our spiritual growth and answers the following questions:

What did the Mayans know about 2012 and why does their calendar end in December of 2012?; Why did the Hopi point to 2012 and say any chance at salvation is now useless as we have gone too far?; Why is there so much fear about 2012?

Isn't it pretty likely there will be one or more disasters in the future?; Is it true that the Earth's population will be reduced to 500 million?; Will Jesus reappear in 2012?; Will aliens rescue the surviving population like a modern Noah's ark?; Are aliens already here?; Is the Earth going to be like a cell dividing in two—people who ascend going with the new Earth and the others staying behind thinking the rest are dead or gone?

Will there be a nuclear war or will the Earth be hit by an asteroid causing an ice age?; Are pole shifts occurring that may cause chaos in 2012? How about solar flares and problems related to that causing Earth disturbances?; Is it true that a civilization will emerge from middle Earth in 2012?; Is overpopulation going to cause a disaster in 2012?

We learn by crisis. Does it appear that we're getting it or do we need bigger and bigger crises to move ahead?; Regarding 2012, are there any safe areas?; If it's true that everyone is going to ascend anyway, what's the point in all the work that we're doing?; How can I deal with my fear and anxiety regarding 2012? Is there anything I should do to prepare for it?; What will happen after 2012?

The book also contains four of Eloheim's tools for spiritual growth: Point fingers; What's in your lap?; What is true now?; and You to you. Additionally, there are 62 definitions of terms and concepts including: ascension, creating your reality, consciousness-based operating system, energetics, ensoulment, free will, Homo spiritus, shadow, soul's perspective, transformation, vibration, and your internal world creates your external experience.

The book closes with information about Eloheim and The Council and a description of the channeling process.

Use the energy of 2012 to facilitate your personal growth!

   —Eloheim

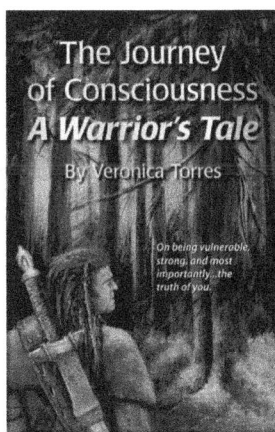

The Journey of Consciousness, A Warrior's Tale

"This entire story is to help you know who you are."

This "fairy tale for grown-ups" follows the Warrior's journey as he encounters castles and kings, battles and beasties, while learning to live from an open heart. The Warrior explains how to live the truth of you, how to have a healthy relationship to authority figures, and how to be vulnerable and strong at the same time.

"Anything that is presenting itself to you is presenting itself to you for growth."

Filled with humor, sage advice, penetrating insight, and above all, profound support for your process, the Warrior's tale clarifies your spiritual path.

"Now, it's really fun to see the King when you stink. Why? Because what you want the king to know is that you are not just a little pawn in his game to be manipulated to his benefit. When you go to see the king, whomever the king is in your world, take who you are with you, and if that means you drop mud on this perfect floor, well, there you are."

◆◆◆

The Warrior is one of the seven Council members channeled by Veronica Torres. The Council's teachings focus on spiritual growth and the movement from the fear-based to the consciousness-based operating system. They specialize in offering specific tools which will facilitate your spiritual growth.

In addition to the Warrior's story, The Journey of Consciousness includes the following tools: Clarity vs. certainty; Feet under shoulders; How ridiculous does it have to get?; I don't know anything; Lay it down and walk away; Mad scientist; Neutral observation; "No" is a complete sentence; Point fingers; Preferences/judgments; Script holding/Script-holders; Strongest chakra; Vulnerability vs. weakness; What's in your lap?; What is true now?; Where am I lying to myself? "Wow!", not "why?", and You to you (comparing). It also includes 126 definitions of terms and concepts used in The Council's teachings.

◆◆◆

"When you're facing your triggers, if you start to waiver in your courage, just imagine that we stand behind you. We stand there to show you that you don't have to fear that you are not enough. You can be afraid of the triggers, but don't be afraid that you're not enough. We will stand beside you in consciousness and courage any time you wish."

—The Warrior

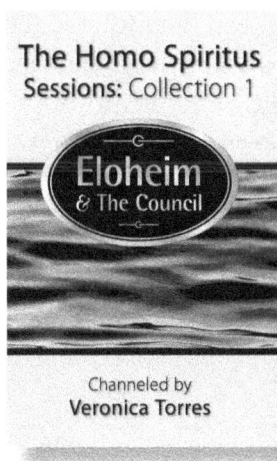

The Homo Spiritus
Sessions: Collection 1

Eloheim
& The Council

Channeled by
Veronica Torres

The Homo Spiritus Sessions, Collection 1

COLLECTION ONE of the *Homo Spiritus Sessions* includes the transcripts of **EIGHT Eloheim and The Council channeling sessions held between July 7, 2010 and August 25, 2010.**

The focus of COLLECTION ONE is:

It's not WHY is this happening? It's WOW this is happening! Experiences are here to facilitate growth, expansion, and transformation. Nothing happens TO you, it all happens FOR you. You create your reality by choosing your reactions to your experiences.

The spiritual journey is a natural process of expansion (growth) and contraction (contemplation). Through this process, you discover the truth of you and learn to emanate that truth into the world. Empower yourself by discerning the difference between vulnerability and weakness. Evolve your relationship to the survival instinct; don't let fear and habits tell you who you are!

The truth of you is emanated into the world through your choices about how you react to your creations. If issues come up again, it doesn't mean you're broken, it means you're going deeper; allow yourself to go deeper with it.

Feelings are not emotions! Feelings are a deep and powerful

pathway to ascension based on what is actually occurring in this moment. Emotions are habitually, biologically, and/or culturally based. Be vulnerable. Tell the truth. Be honest about your feelings. Be willing to admit when you want to learn something. Open to the fact that you don't know everything.

When you're tempted to be in the past or the future, we invite you to say: "Am I courageous enough to be with me now? Am I courageous enough to attend to my concerns about me? My fascination about me. My insight about me. Am I courageous enough to do that?"

Where do you feel unlovable? The answer is the doorway to the next level of your spiritual growth. The true nature of your infinite, and immortal self resides just a breath away in any moment, and it exists for you to access at any time.

The *Homo Spiritus Sessions* series offers channeled messages from Eloheim and The Council.

The Council is comprised of seven different groups: The Guardians, The Girls, The Visionaries, The Matriarch, The Eloheim, The Warrior, and Fred. During a channeling session, each of The Council members take turns sharing their teachings. Each Council member has a distinct personality, style of delivery, and focus.

The Council is best known for their multitude of practical tools, which support our journey out of the fear-based operating system into the consciousness-based operating system.

COLLECTION ONE includes 29 tools:

Big toe, left elbow; Choose and choose again; Color with all the crayons; Don't be mean to yourself; Equal signs; Feelings are not emotions; Feet under shoulders; Go to the bathroom; How ridiculous does it have to get?; Mad Scientist; Money mantra; Neutral observation; "No" is a complete sentence; Point fingers; Preferences/Judgments; Re-queue; Script holding; Short, factual statements; Velcro; Vulnerability vs. weakness; What is in your lap?; What is IS; What is true now?; Where am I lying to myself?; Who answers the door?; Why, why, why?; Wow!, not why?; You can't have change without change; You to you (compare).

Additionally, COLLECTION ONE includes 126 definitions of terms and concepts.

Each of the *Homo Spiritus Sessions* books can stand alone, but taken together will allow the reader to follow along with the progression of the teachings including the introduction, in-depth explanation, and evolution of The Council's tools.

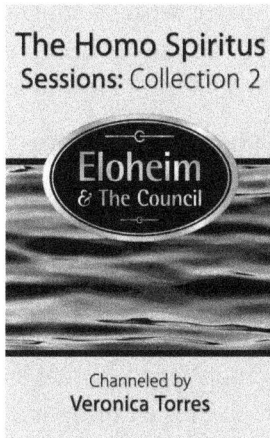

The Homo Spiritus Sessions, Collection 2

COLLECTION TWO of the *Homo Spiritus Sessions* includes transcripts of EIGHT Eloheim and The Council channeling sessions held between September 1, 2010 and October 20, 2010.

The focus of COLLECTION TWO is:

You can't say no to the truth of you because it makes other people uncomfortable.

Contemplation of your inner self emanates your truth. Take the time and make the effort to find things to love about yourself, no matter how mundane they may seem. Your soul cannot access the places where you don't love yourself.

Only compare you to you. Find even the smallest measurable amount that feels like progress. It doesn't have to be stupendous to be something wonderful.

In the same way that you can choose to change your physical body through exercise or lifting weights, you can choose to change your life by attending to your triggers. Form a new relationship to triggers in order to become a better friend to yourself.

Your outer world is a reflection of your inner self. You "put the film in the camera" and see what is shown "on the screen" of your life. It can't get to the movie screen unless you put it in the camera.

COLLECTION TWO includes 28 tools:
Big toe, left elbow; Clarity vs. certainty; Color with all the crayons; Equal signs; Feelings are not emotions; Film in the camera; How ridiculous does it have to get?; I don't know anything; Lay it down and walk away; Look for the wink; Look out the window; Money mantra; Neutral observation; Preferences/ Judgments; Script holding; Short, factual statements; Shovel or ladder; Superhero powers; This emotion is a choice; This is happening for me; Velcro; Vulnerability vs. weakness; What am I afraid of?; What is in your lap?; What is true now?; Who answers the door?; You can't have change without change; and You to you (compare).

Additionally, COLLECTION TWO includes 131 definitions of terms and concepts including the new terms: Fred's portal and Monk in the marketplace.

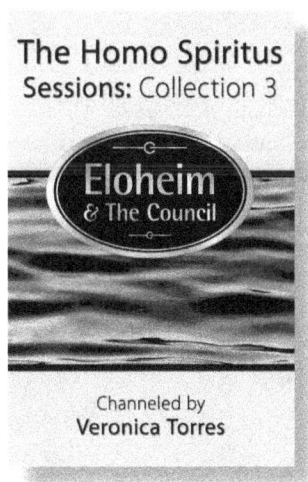

The Homo Spiritus Sessions, Collection 3

COLLECTION THREE of *The Homo Spiritus Sessions* includes transcripts of EIGHT Eloheim and The Council channeling sessions held between October 27, 2010 and December 15, 2010.

The focus of COLLECTION THREE is:

The focus of the spiritual journey is, "I want healing above all else." The path of healing includes learning how to be comfortable in "I don't know." It's very rare to abide in "I don't know" comfortably, yet that is the place where all revelation occurs. Until you decide you don't know it all, there's nothing more you can learn.

Look for the places where you want to hide from your truth. Uncertainty will bring you into the moment and uncertainty with the moment will take you into Homo spiritus on the path of ascension.

You show people how to love you by the way you love yourself, and by the way you love yourself you will be known. Respect yourself enough to set boundaries and love yourself enough to be kind to yourself as you're doing it.

COLLECTION THREE includes 34 tools:
Big toe, left elbow; Candle wax; Choose and choose again; Clarity vs. certainty; Color with all the crayons; Don't be mean to yourself; Equal signs; Feelings are not emotions; Film in the camera; How ridiculous does it have to get?; I don't know anything; I'm tempted to; Lay it down and walk away; Look for the wink; Look out the window; Money mantra; Neutral observation; Preferences/Judgments; Re-queue; Script holding; Short, factual statements; Shovel or ladder; Strongest chakra; Superhero powers; This emotion is a choice; This is happening for me; Velcro; Vulnerability vs. weakness; What am I afraid of?; What is in your lap?; What is true now?; Who answers the door?; You can't have change without change; and You to you (compare).

Additionally, COLLECTION THREE includes 131 definitions of terms and concepts.

The Homo Spiritus
Sessions: Collection 4

Eloheim
& The Council

Channeled by
Veronica Torres

The Homo Spiritus Sessions, Collection 4

COLLECTION FOUR of *The Homo Spiritus Sessions* includes transcripts of EIGHT Eloheim and The Council channeling sessions held between December 22, 2010 and February 9, 2011.

The focus of COLLECTION FOUR is:

Being uncertain is your nature. Striving for certainty leads you to be mean to yourself. Whenever you want certainty, you're setting yourself up to fail.

Your soul wants to experience everything there is to experience, living in fear and always striving for safety closes you to many experiences.

Make peace with uncertainty to experience serenity.

When you look at the field of infinite possibilities, what do you think is possible but not possible for you? Where you put your attention creates a force of attraction for your intention. What you're attentive to creates in your life.

COLLECTION FOUR includes 22 tools:

Candle wax; Clarity vs. certainty; Color with all the crayons; Equal signs; Feelings are not emotions; How ridiculous does it have to get?; I'm tempted to; Neutral observation; Point fingers; Preferences/Judgments; Re-queue; Script holding; Short, factual statements; This is happening for me; Vulnerability vs. weakness; What am I afraid of?; What is in your lap?; What is is; What is true now?; Where are you lying to yourself?; You can't have change without change; and You to you (compare).

Additionally, COLLECTION FOUR includes 134 definitions of terms and concepts including the new terms: Healing above all else, I'm willing, and Spilling the orange juice.

www.ingramcontent.com/pod-product-compliance
Lightning Source LLC
Chambersburg PA
CBHW020505030426

42337CB00011B/234